Karma and reincarnation go hand in hand as the logical explanation of why a man comes into this life either blessed or burdened with the pattern shown in his Birth Chart; a pattern which shows the degree of growth of his soul through countless incarnations and the necessity of the experiences he must know in his present life if he is to continue to make progress.

from Chapter 1,
"Astrology Answers Why"

ASTROLOGY

KEY TO SELF

ASTROLOGY

KEY TO SELF-UNDERSTANDING

UNDERSTANDING

YOUR GUIDE TO ESOTERIC ASTROLOGY, REINCARNATION AND KARMA

Leonora K. Luxton

1978
Llewellyn Publications
St. Paul, Minnesota 55164

First Edition 1978

Llewellyn Publications
Post Office Box 43383
Saint Paul, Minnesota 55164

International Standard Book Number: 0-87542-331-0

Typographer: Chester-Kent, Inc., St. Paul, MN
Lithographer: R. R. Donnelley & Sons Co., Chicago, IL

To Earl, for his faith in this book, and to Faith Javane and Martha Christopher for help in its preparation.

Contents

Preface

At a time when many are questioning old teachings and seeking in new ways some clearer insight into man's relation to God, astrology, the oldest of the sciences, takes on a greater meaning, and through it man comes to an understanding of his place in the world and of his soul as part of the Oversoul.

Many textbooks have been offered the student to prove that astrology works and to give the rules for preparing the natal chart and interpreting the effect of aspects to planets therein; but it is not enough to know the technique and standardized interpretation of planets in signs and houses. The definite correspondence between the time when certain planets form precise angular aspects to natal planets and the results which come to pass at such times ought to convince the most skeptical that force or vibrations directed from planetary bodies in various ways influence the etheric body and therefore the emotional attitudes of all living creatures.

What seems most needed today is not an understanding of *how* astrology works, but *why*. Like every science, astrology must be expanded continuously as new planets are discovered and the complexities of man's civilization call for more varied interpretations of planetary influence in the many facets of each life. Unwillingness to consider a new planetary ruler for some sign now assigned to a planet ruling a more compatible sign results in lack of accurate interpretation, since predictions based on incorrect rulerships cannot work, and in such instances astrology, rather than the astrologer, may be discredited.

This book, therefore, offers to the student and professional ideas which contradict or differ from those of old authorities, yet which give astrology a greater meaning, since through deeper understanding of the nature of signs and planets the reader comes to know clearly not simply how astrology works, but why.

It presents astrology not simply as a predictive technique, through which conditions in the present life may be foreknown, but as the way in which the individual may reach a better understanding of the reason for the soul's eternal life and its repeated return to earthly experience.

It traces the nature of the soul's evolving path from mortal life to highest spiritual truth through all the zodiacal signs. It shows how in each sign some needed experience must be gained, so that in time the three non-material principles descended from the Omnipotent Whole may so evolve on the spiral path that they are freed of the necessity for incarnation and merged with the Highest Potential.

It seeks to tell the reader why life is necessary for the growth of spiritual principles, including man's immortal soul, why the soul must continue to return many times for added life experience, why some are born into conditions of great difficulty while others know only luxury or ease, and how each man makes for himself the pattern of succeeding life experiences.

Lastly, it interprets astrology as philosophy in addition to showing it as the most logical of techniques through which the student may arrive at self-understanding and a preview of conditions in the present life.

Acknowledgements

Many chapters in this unorthodox approach to astrology resulted from the generous personal suggestions of the late George E. Jordan, to whom I am deeply indebted for many concepts of interpretation not available to either the student or the professional astrologer.

Through the past decade I have freely offered some of these suggestions to classes and professionals with the thought that by testing them a further awareness of their importance might be gained. I wish to thank those who have ventured to include these interpretations in their class instruction.

Chapters on disputed rulerships of some signs contain material previously printed in other forms in the *Bulletin of the American Federation of Astrologers,* since I desired to put very controversial material before a wider group of professional members of the national association.

Finally, I wish to express my sincere appreciation to Faith Javane of Dover, New Hampshire, and Martha Christopher of Boston for their assistance in typing some of the several revisions and final copy, and to my husband, Earl, for his continued encourgement.

1
Astrology Answers 'Why?'

More than three decades ago, in my early days as a professional astrologer, I ventured to offer those interested in astrology a popular book under the title, *Follow Your Lucky Stars* (Philadelphia: Penn Publishing Co., 1940), using the charts of prominent personalities of the thirties to illustrate the exactness with which astrological aspects show times of outstanding success or disaster.

Published under the pen name of Nona Howard, under which I then wrote for *Horoscope Magazine* and many lesser astrological publications, it advised readers to take advantage of fortunate aspects from Jupiter, Venus and Uranus to start those ventures in which they hoped for success, but to delay and resist changes when their natal charts showed adverse aspects from transiting or progressed planets.

Such advice still seems to be the reason for astrology's appeal to millions. True, astrology is an invaluable guide to times of difficulty, periods of opportunity, occasions when one may find fortune changing in an unexpected way. It permits the individual to take advantage of favorable conditions and protect against recurrent transits which impose increased responsibilities or delay progress.

But many years of research, practice and application have greatly changed my concept of why astrology is important to everyone and why another kind of book seems justified.

This is not meant to be a textbook; rather it seeks to confirm what Henry Ward Beecher once wrote: "The practical application of astrology should interest every human being who cares to rise above the common level of humanity. Its value is that it does for the human race what no other science pretends to do, and this is to show man his proper place in life."

Astrology does more than this if the student correctly interprets the esoteric and philosophical lessons to be learned through a study of the personal chart. It shows each individual the reasons for his present condition in life, the degree of spiritual progress made by his eternal soul in former periods of incarnation and the plan to be followed in the present life if further evolutionary growth is to proceed. It is, too, an x-ray of the individual and the answer to that often heard question, *Why do we live?*

Briefly, astrology is truth, and the competent astrologer must practice the art of interpreting truth. Astrology asks the student to accept what science knows–that in all things there is a law of cause and effect. In the eastern world, this is called karma. Karma works without deviation from the lowest form of life to the final and formless state of mortal integration with the highest.

Source, from the first incarnation of the eternal monad through all incarnations, since no period of mortal life offers the individual sufficient opportunities to correct all errors of conduct made in the present or during past lives nor to receive the rewards gained from doing good to others.

Karma and reincarnation go hand in hand as the logical explanation of why a man comes into this life either blessed or burdened with the pattern shown in his birth chart; this pattern shows the degree of growth of his soul through countless incarnations and the necessity of the experiences he must know in his present life if he is to continue to make progress.

When astrologers speak of the monad, they refer to what has been defined as a microscopic embodiment of the Divine Essence which man calls God, which pervades and constitutes the universe. Therefore, the spiritual life atoms that are a part of this Oneness are sometimes spoken of as the "divine sparks."

The continuity of individuality of these spiritual life atoms, which in many eons of time descend to form life and function within the physical body, may be observed by studying the birth chart of those no longer physically embodied. Long after life terminates, aspects to the natal Sun, which is the spiritual monad in a chart, continue to produce effects in connection with that personality. Form perishes, but the monad lives on. If the natal chart of someone long dead is observed, it will be found that what is at that time written or said of that person reflects the aspect to the Sun. Many examples of this could be offered in proof of the eternal life of the monad, but while religion accepts some form of eternal life, the western world seems reluctant to think that we return again and again to mortal form, and asks both whether reincarnation is possible and why it is necessary.

The answer may be seen in nature—the necessity of continued growth. For man, this is the growth from the monad, the seed atom which comes in time to function in physical form, through involution from spirit to mental principle, then into etheric or astral form and finally into what man calls physical form, through which experience may be gained in the many circumstances of life.

Nature proves the necessity of continuous growth from seed to mature plant, reproduction of seed for future life, and then physical decay or destruction of the previous form. Man follows this same process of involution from spiritual or highest form in which the monad is individualized to lowest or mortal form. But when human form reaches its fullest development through many periods of life experience, etheric form is released in the moment of physical death and with it the mental principle and spiritual monad pass to planes of higher vibration.

Nothing is permanent except change, but through continuous change man is promoted from the classroom of earth to a plane from which truly evolved souls or discarnate minds may make contact with mortal minds, influence their thought and, in service to those who are less aware, give some spiritual understanding gained through their own life and postlife experience.

Should a soul so freed from physical incarnation lack

sufficient development to serve those less evolved, however, there is an absolute necessity for reincarnation and continued life experience, since no discarnate soul is released from the wheel of life until every lesson has been learned through mundane experience. What cycle of schooling has been reached, as well as the nature of further lessons required, can be seen clearly in each child's birth chart.

In the natural sequence of the signs the student may see the order of the courses through which spiritual monads learn all needed lessons and what progress has been made, for in the present life the position of the Sun in the chart indicates the point the individual has reached. One may know through the horoscope, therefore, both the reason for return to mortal life and the degree of development the soul has reached through many past lives.

While the natal horoscope is the pattern for each life, free will permits the individual to decide whether he makes the utmost progress under the conditions he has earned, or whether he ceases to grow by failure to accept the challenges in his horoscope. Unless he follows this pattern, however difficult, he may reach only a limited fulfillment of the monad's capacity for growth, for only through the desire of each individual for fullest accomplishment can progress be made. In each life the monad is reborn into situations fortunate or otherwise, but always those which are earned by past conduct, because the law of karma operates with the utmost justice. Some desire for progress is always present because, in the monad, the creative will always aspires to ascend from the physical shell in which it is imprisoned to ultimate freedom from physical life, and highest spiritual attainment–Nirvana, the merging with All Wisdom.

If this desire and will to progress is strong, progress will be made in proportion to desire, not in relation to opportunity or the circumstances of life. The individual birth chart shows the strength of desire, as well as the opportunity offered for constructive growth. Whether astrology is seen as a pattern for the present life or an interval of experience in the soul's progress toward its ultimate goal, it offers greater guidance than other sciences.

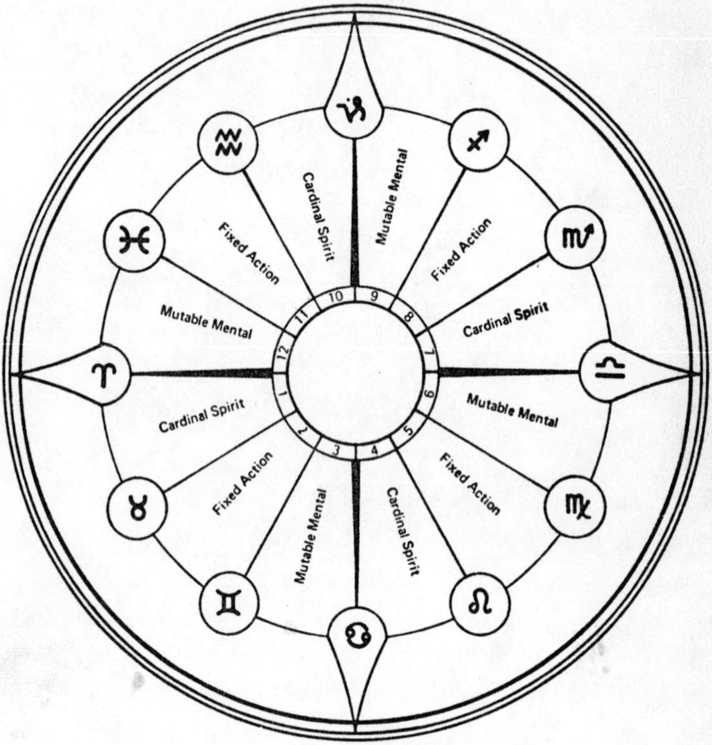

Judging the Chart

2
Judging the Chart

Before the student of astrology comes to a decision regarding the nature of any individual whose chart is under consideration, he must consider, in addition to the position of the Sun by sign and house, and the dispositor ruling the Sun Sign, the number of planets in each sign and whether such planets are fixed, mutable, or cardinal.

Through this observation one can discover whether the individual will act, think, or merely change inwardly as the result of every transit or transiting aspect. Those who have many planets in the fixed signs take action and are conditioned by circumstances and change of circumstance. Any chart in which there are many planets in fixed signs is that of the individual who will do far more than one who has planets in mutable (mental) or cardinal (spiritual) signs.

The cardinal type is a leader insofar as he initiates action through ideas, but unless he also has a number of planets in fixed signs, he is unlikely to carry out that action personally. He initiates activity which can be carried out by another.

In the mutable signs, the activity takes place on the mental plane. Many things of great importance may be in the mind of a man, but unless that mind coordinates thought with deeds, as the result of planets in fixed signs in the chart, there is likely to be much thinking but little action.Therefore, before any chart may be seen as that of an individual who will act, it is necessary to judge the quality of the majority of signs in that chart.

If, as sometimes happens, the chart shows a rather even balance of signs in each of the three qualities, it may be judged the birth map of a well-balanced individual, able to originate activity through the cardinal signs in his chart, think out what course of action to take through the planets in the mutable group of signs, and then act as the result of the planets in fixed signs.

Such balanced charts are those of individuals who may accomplish much, since they are well organized within themselves, work to carry forward what they conceive, and put ideas into plans that may be expressed through deeds.

The chart with many planets in cardinal signs may have the great quality of inner awareness and spiritual growth, but fail to express this in what is said or written, and almost never in action, unless some strongly placed planet in a fixed sign compels such action. This type of individual lives within himself, does not seek to gain attention, and if left completely alone, may seem very inactive. All experience is internal and therefore unobserved by the world. Such a man is poorly qualified to function on the material level because he cannot express what is deeply within his soul through his mind (if there are less than a couple of planets in the mutable signs), and even less take decisive action, due to the lack of planets in fixed signs. To the outsider, this individual will seem to have few experiences, though within himself he may feel and react to every type of situation.

Such a man will not make many drastic changes in the course of his life. Those which come about as the result of progressions and transits take place inwardly, and changes of circumstances which compel him to deviate from his usual attitude affect him within far more than without. No matter how abnormal these circumstances may become, they seem to leave his life unchanged. A chart of this type is not that of a man of great achievement, though it may be that of one who has lived through many incarnations and made fine inner growth. It is much easier for the student to interpret the chart in which action is indicated.

Somewhat the same situation results when a chart is heavy with mutable signs. Such a man lives within his mind, and circumstances act upon the mind to change the mental attitude. In a sense, the mind is master of the man, for only through the mind is he able to express himself.

This could be the chart of a great writer, for the writer expresses through what the mind creates. A man may have a great thought, but unless that thought results in action or words written or spoken, the world seldom knows it was worth thinking.

With these principles in mind, consider, as an example, the chart of a man who accomplished much. In

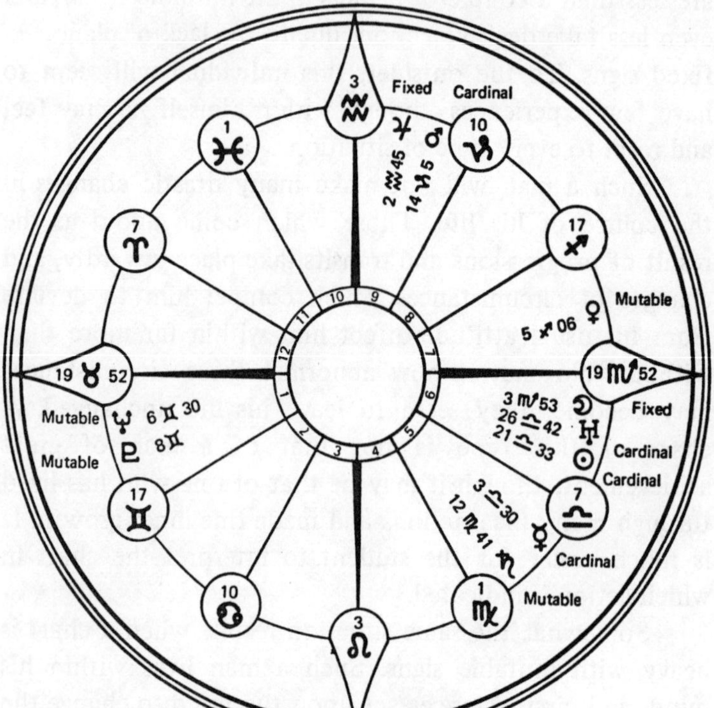

Dwight D. Eisenhower
October 14, 1890, 6:49 pm
Denison, Texas

this chart there are several planets in fixed signs, many in mutable and a few in cardinal, revealing a man who expressed the quality of spirit through the mind and then through action taken under circumstances which resulted in change, development and personal accomplishment observable to the whole world.

The chart is that of a former president of the United States, Dwight D. Eisenhower, born in Denison, Texas, on October 14, 1890. In this chart there is a fairly well-balanced segment translating the quality of the inner self into ideas, and thus into activity resulting in great accomplishment in the eyes of the world. Eisenhower has Jupiter in a fixed sign, Aquarius, almost on the cusp of the tenth house. What the world remembers him for must be something of a rather outstanding and unusual nature, since Aquarius brings the unexpected and out of the ordinary. Not only was he president, but also, as a result of circumstances in World War II, he was the man who led the victorious troops in the D-Day invasion against the Nazi forces and brought to an end that terrible global conflict.

Like Ulysses S. Grant, Dwight D. Eisenhower is much more likely to be remembered for this than for his less important service to his country as its president. So truly Uranian in its unexpectedness was his contribution in the D-Day landings that, until the final hours, only those in the highest military positions in the Allied armies knew what was impending.

In Eisenhower's birth chart is the indication that this man would draw to himself many men who thought him a great leader, and who had confidence to accept from him decisions that changed the course of the world's history.

This is why, in the various charts that come to astrologers, we may see that some men are leaders, others are doers who act only through necessity (as a result of having many natal planets in fixed signs), and others accomplish almost nothing, but have gained great strength of soul through many lives, coming finally to the highest pinnacle of spiritual growth.

A chart filled with planets in the fixed signs is the chart of someone who is always active, always doing something on the material level. This is also the chart of one who will experience so many changes of circumstances that it should be simple to predict such changes, for *activity is the observable result of every aspect formed to the planets in fixed signs.*

Because of this great difference in the way various individuals react to transits, the astrologer may be badly misled if predictions are made solely on the basis of the old rules for results. Much less can be expected to happen if the chart under consideration is one with more planets in cardinal or mental signs than in the signs which are expressed through action.

These action-type charts are not, of course, charts which indicate much continued development along lines of inner growth, but rather those of continual change. Such persons grow as the result of experience. This is particularly true if as many as four or more planets are in signs which demand action. Such an individual may in a few hours do something which results in changes that effect his life for many years in the future. He tends to demand instant decisions, in spite of intelligent thought and often without reason, simply to stimulate activity on the part of others.

To return to the consideration of the well-balanced chart of Eisenhower: he has four of ten planets in cardinal or spiritual signs. He has four planets in mutable or mental signs and two in the group which results in action, but action strongly backed by the inner quality of leadership and the mental ability to translate this quality into thought. Two planets in fixed signs result in activity stimulated by both the mind and the spirit.

Such a chart indicates a man who has developed himself to a degree which gives him the status to lead others, and to make such tremendous decisions in regard to the lives of other men as Eisenhower was forced to make before D-Day. It shows the type of mind capable of making decisions for forthright and immediate action. Mercury is in Libra, a cardinal sign, but Venus, the dispositor of Mercury, is in Sagittarius, in his seventh house of contacts with the public and open enemies. Thus in dealing with both the public and his opponents, he deals in a highly intelligent, almost inspired, way. His Mercury is in close trine, a most fortunate aspect, to Pluto and Neptune, both in the practical mental sign of Gemini. Neptune gives him the psychic link with the spiritual plane, and Pluto enables him to destroy old concepts and ideas and to recreate them on a higher level. The fact that both planets are in a most fortunate aspect to practical Mercury, in the sign which balances and weighs ideas, made him capable of tuning in more widely to the mass-mind than other men, since Pluto rules large groups, not merely individuals.

When Eisenhower had to decide whether to make the move that could have cost so heavily in men's lives that day, yet might, if it succeeded, save many more lives by bringing the war to an immediate conclusion, he was thinking in terms of what the world's war-ravaged peoples might will him to do, not merely what this invasion might mean to a few military leaders. His mind, backed by a spiritual growth that may be seen in those four birth planets in cardinal signs, was able to meet such a test.

In the final illustration of how Neptune and Pluto in Gemini, trine Mercury in Libra, operated in the personality of this great military leader, observe how Jupiter forms a grand trine, to bring success as the result of thought and inner awareness. Jupiter in a fixed sign resulted in unexpected action. But being able to act as the result of combined spiritual and mental ability, Eisenhower was able to do the spectacular, yet only after he had weighed every possible result.

In reading any chart, after the student surveys the whole natal map to determine the balance of planets according to quality, he should concentrate on the particular planet under consideration and note the sign in which the planet is placed. But he must always go one step beyond this and note the dispositor of the sign in which this particular planet may be. Only in this way is it possible to appreciate the modification and special coloring the planet gives.

There is a great difference between the way Pluto acts

in Taurus, a fixed sign, and in Gemini, a mutable one. In Taurus, Pluto's destructive action is in connection with circumstances. In Gemini, a mutable sign, it acts through mental attitudes. In Mercury's sign Pluto seeks to destroy old ideas and concepts in order to recreate them on a higher level. In Cancer the destruction is more an inner experience than either mentally or actively expressed.

Pluto in Leo destroys all old matters ruled by the fifth house sign in the national chart, while in Virgo it does away with many former mental attitudes in connection with all sixth house, Virgo-ruled matters—particularly service and labor.

For the most complete understanding of the way any planet will act, therefore, the student should consider the nature of the dispositor as well as the nature of the sign in which the planet may be at the birth, since this is almost as important for full interpretation. To do less would be to judge the chart on a basis of incomplete facts.

3
The Art of Interpretation

Although the drawing of an astrological chart is a well-established process and interpretation is based on rules formulated over many centuries, horoscopy is still considered an art, depending, as it does, upon the skill of the interpreter to synthesize the many factors which enter into any judgment. The astrologer can master this phase of the subject if he is able to evaluate the effect of *all* aspects at once. These must include natal, progressed, and transiting, since all must be in agreement, or at least indicate conditions of the same nature at the approximate date for which the chart is considered.

Since all aspects must be appraised, the student should first observe those resulting from radical aspects (those which exist in the chart at the time of birth), as these show the potentials for future conditions of the nature they indicate. Then, if he seeks to predict the time when potential events will come to pass, he must consider both progressed and transiting aspects in the chart, because they are closely interrelated.

He must understand so well the correspondence

between transits and the much slower progressions that he can determine with exactness periods of great opportunity or great risk, as well as conditions which could effect the well-being of the individual, his family, his fortune and the opinion which the world may have of him.

If, for example, the radical chart shows that at some time in life the individual will suffer from the disruptive or unfortunate effects of a planet in unfavorable relation to another planet in the natal chart, this condition can only come to pass when the degree and the sign position of this planet is caught between the progressed aspect and the culminating or corresponding transiting aspect of major planets and confirmed by minor ones.

Suppose there is a Mars square Jupiter aspect in the birth chart. Such an aspect potentially indicates an individual who must suffer from legal action or from the law, unless Jupiter is so well aspected that the favorable aspects can overcome the disruptive ones. When there is a corresponding aspect to Mars or Jupiter, brought about by slow progression, plus aspects of the same nature formed by the transiting major and minor planets, then this conflict with what Jupiter rules takes shape, both because it is indicated in the natal chart and because it is brought about by corresponding progressions confirmed by transits. It is important to realize, however, that if this aspect of legal difficulties did *not* exist in the chart at the time of birth, progressions plus transits would not cause it to come to pass.

The individual with an adverse aspect of a malefic planet to Jupiter is not always in trouble with the law, but should he have Jupiter unfavorably aspected by Mars and then have another unfriendly planet transit, the condition will at this time be brought into action.

While progressions are also important in timing, only the Sun, Moon, Mercury, Venus and Mars make progressed aspects to very many planets in a lifetime. The student must therefore check both progressed (if any) and transiting aspects and their agreement in order to verify indications of disruptive, unfortunate, favorable or unexpected developments.

In connection with predictions, it is also necessary to observe the quality of the chart– that is, whether the nature of the sign in which both the transiting and progressed planets are placed is cardinal, mutable or fixed. If the coinciding aspects are in fixed signs and aspect a natal planet in a cardinal sign, the effect will be felt within rather than through a change of circumstances. Therefore, there might not seem to be any real result, even though the individual will feel keenly at this time the effect of the experience.

On the other hand, if the transiting aspects take place in the fixed signs, events will come to pass which are so obvious that they manifest in an unmistakable way.

Since every chart receives, often at the same time, both fortunate and unfortunate aspects, no one should see disruptive experience as the only thing which can happen under conditions suggesting some undesirable kind of event. Many students tend to think that astrology shows only the disasters, never the fortunate opportunities. Actually, the birth chart shows all that is, was, or will be in any life. As may be seen in the aspects to the natal Sun in the charts of the famous, aspects formed to the position of the Sun continue to bring such persons into the news long after death, favorably or otherwise, according to the nature of the aspect to their Sun at birth in the latest incarnation.

Sometimes a transit will show a fortunate aspect at a time when the individual or others may consider conditions most unfortunate: if, for instance, he failed to recover from a long and painful illness and died under such a transit. But should there be favorable aspects at that time to the natal Sun in the chart, as sometimes happens, death will bring only favorable attention from the world and greater honor to the individual.

Many of the aspects which form to the Sun in a chart affect what is within rather than the conditions of outer life, unless in the chart the Sun is in a fixed sign and rules the ascendant. In such cases, it is the personality rather than the inner self which reflects the changes that progressed and transiting aspects bring about.

Transits to the ruler of the ascendant must always result in changes of the personal attitude or personality, because the ruler of the ascendant indicates the personality of the individual. In other transits or aspects, study the house ruled by the planet forming the aspect and the planet aspected, as well as its house position in the birth chart, to discover where the effect of the transit or progressed aspect will be felt in the life.

It is regrettable that often the student or professional

looks primarily for signs of disaster rather than for improved conditions in a chart, or fails to see good aspects strong enough to outweigh or offset any disruptive ones. All too frequently, he tends to concentrate too heavily on Mars' accidental, or Saturn's delaying or disappointing influences, if these are observed as impending by transit, and in so doing, he fails to give to the client all information the chart shows, thereby discouraging him needlessly. At the same time, those who interpret aspects ought to explain that, in a sense, aspects show the working out of that wise observation, "One cannot have everything," for there is almost no such situation as complete good fortune without any disadvantage, nor of utter disaster void of compensation of one kind or another.

To interpret a chart adequately, the basis of interpretation must be a *complete* appreciation of all aspects operating at a given time; the interpreter must not be ninety percent right and ten percent wrong. This can happen by failing to observe that, in spite of an unfavorable transit of some planet like Neptune, which causes deception, misrepresentation or fraud, there is also a beneficent aspect of a planet like Jupiter culminating at the same period, bringing benefit from legal aid.

The student should bear this in mind at all times, and look at *every* aspect, not merely the bad ones. By and large, there are no truly bad aspects, but simply aspects that are disruptive and delaying, which demand stamina and fortitude to bear. By accepting continually increasing burdens, man becomes more aware of his own ability to carry this weight.

When the chart shows an aspect indicating the termination of life, even this is not always a malefic aspect. Often death comes when the chart shows neither unfavorable progressions nor transits. For many, it is a door to a far greater and better world, and some charts clearly show this. To consider death only as the result of evil aspects is far from competent interpretation. For some it can be a great reward or freedom from a life far less desirable.

A chart showing many planets in mutable signs and afflicted by unfavorable aspects may still permit the individual to live in good health and be financially prosperous, but with a mind forced to carry great burdens of responsibility, disrupted by conflict and controversy.

The result will likewise differ if the afflicted planets are in cardinal signs. In such circumstances the individual knows such inner testing, such a struggle for supremacy between the finer quality of the soul and the nature of the self, that he is really tormented, though to the world his life may appear completely normal.

The importance, therefore, of considering the quality of the chart before attempting to predict how any aspect may work out is never to be forgotten.

For example, conflict may come about because Mars in aspect to any planet suggests drastic and aggressive action. But if Mars is passing through a cardinal sign, such action is against the inner nature, and is only against the person if Mars at the time is aspecting a cardinal sign planet ruling the ascendant. Should Mars show aspects of the same nature to planets in fixed signs or transit a part of the chart ruled by a fixed sign, however, it will exert positive force against planets that function on the physical level. Therefore, accidents could be feared, since they take place when aggression is directed against physical form or substance.

Since Saturn is the consolidator, the foundation, the director of predetermined and past-determined potentials which man builds during long periods of life, Saturn transits are far better than Mars for many, for this planet gives stability and puts the strength of stone under the whole structure. Those things which result from Saturn aspects come into being as the result of time, discipline, restriction and necessity. Saturn may renew and review old conditions and bring them about in better and more consolidated form, since all enduring things mature only through the process of time, which Saturn rules.

The student should not come to the conclusion that a simple aspect of transiting Saturn is sufficient by itself to cause a great deal of responsibility and therefore to be considered malefic. Saturn is like the cement poured into forms, to set and harden and prepare a foundation for future use in building anything of enduring nature. A transit of Saturn ought, for this reason, to be seen as the preparation for a greater future, for without the Saturn quality of conditioning there is no important development possible.

Neither does giving astrological advice always mean giving warning. It means offering a preview of every condition coming to pass. With such foreknowledge, a man may prepare himself to accept increased responsibility, and also to take advantage of the opportunity or good fortune which may be close at hand, to offset any added burden and mitigate whatever condition results from Saturn's discipline.

The greatest value of astrology is that it reveals truth. Truth, though pictured as blind, is so only because many bandage their own eyes to all but what they wish to see. Therefore the astrologer should be willing to tell the whole truth, not merely a part of it, to those who seek astrological guidance. The client suffers if he knows only the ill fortune impending, since in such cases he lives in fear; yet it is just as unfair to him to point out only the good fortune, if the chart indicates at the same time unfavorable conditions. Without knowledge of these, the tendency is to overexpand and fail to prepare for the less fortunate situations.

Rightly used, prediction of future conditions is the greatest gift the astrologer can offer those who consult him, for through this God gives to all men a preview of what lies ahead; thus, they may mitigate disaster through intelligent foreknowledge or recognize opportunity when it comes. Astrology does not reveal all the minute details of what can be expected. It shows trends only. But the nature of those trends and the time when they will manifest themselves offer more perfect guidance than any other form of prediction, when interpreted by one who fully understands what each planet does by progression and transit.

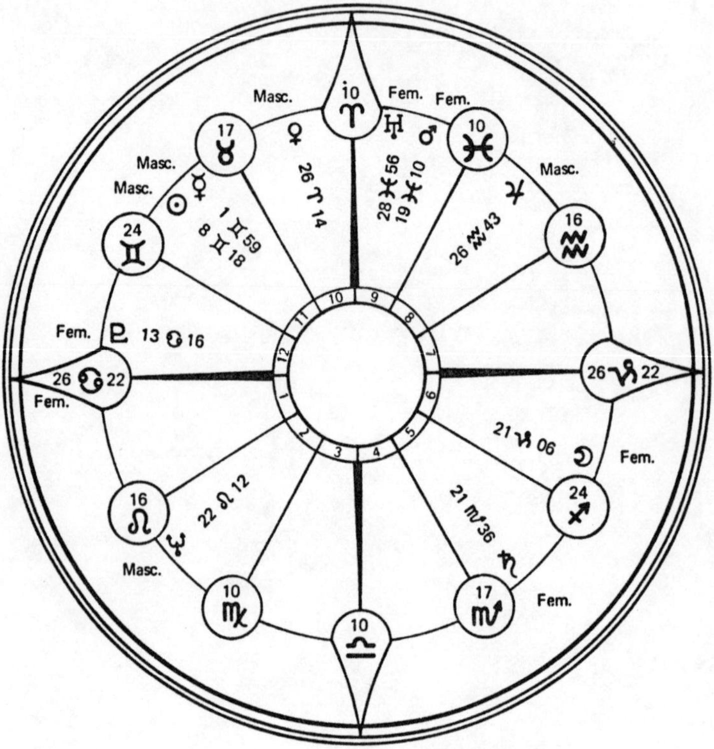

Christine Jorgensen
May 30, 1926, around 9 am

4
Keys to the Personality

For many centuries, during which knowledge has been gained through the study of charts compared to the individuals for whom they were drawn, certain observations have been made that throw much light upon the personality as the birth chart reveals it.

Not without reason have various signs been considered masculine or feminine, positive or negative, since the positive or negative nature of the subject of the chart is indicated with astonishing accuracy by the nature of birth-chart planets in signs of one type or another.

Probably the most unusual example of this correspondence between the nature of natal planets and the personality of the subject is found in the birth horoscope of George Jorgensen. In his twenties, Mr. Jorgensen decided that he was so ill-suited to the sex into which he was born that he submitted to three remarkable operations which altered his physical sexual characteristics, changing him from a very effeminate male into a handsome and fairly acceptable female.

The intimate story of all the reasons why such a

change seemed vitally necessary to him and how it was brought about was published in a frank autobiography, in which the date of birth and dates of many important occasions in his life were given. The time of birth and the place were given over a television network, making this unusual horoscope available for astrological research.

In this chart, the female sign Cancer rules the ascendant, but a point of importance is that the decan ruler is Pisces, suggesting that the appearance is somehow deceptive and not the real nature of the personality. For camouflaged under physical male sex characteristics are five planets astrology classifies as feminine and negative, plus a feminine sign on the ascendant, in a female decan of that sign.

From his earliest memories George Jorgensen had no interest in matters in which most boys delight, but preferred those things regarded as typically feminine. The female sign Virgo rules the third house, and his mental interests were therefore those of a woman. His sexual nature is shown by the restrictive Saturn in Scorpio in the creative fifth house, and in a physical sense this was also true. Pluto, which rules the fifth house, is the destroyer of whatever condition originally existed in any department of the life. In view of the surgical destruction of the original sex characteristics, it is revealing to notice how Pluto is trined by Mars (surgery) in the ninth house. The operations transforming him from male to female took place in Sweden, starting in the fall of 1951, when transiting Uranus, ruling Pluto's natural Scorpio house, was conjunct natal Pluto in this chart. At that time he also

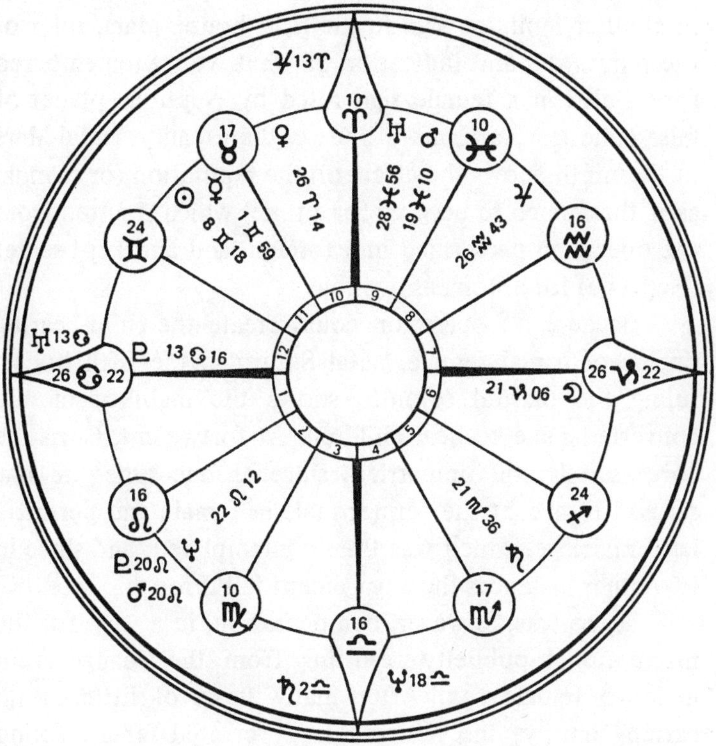

Christine Jorgensen
Transits for fall, 1951—time of
sex change operation

changed his name from George to Christine.

The Moon in a feminine sign is disposited by Saturn in another feminine sign in the fifth house. Mars, ruler of the reputation and indication of what we are remembered for, is also in a female sign ruled by Neptune, planet of false conditions and more illusion than reality. Natal Mars in the ninth shows the effect on the reputation (or scandal as it threatened to become for a time) which resulted from the operation performed in a foreign land and kept secret (Neptune) for as long as possible.

Because no operation could create the child-bearing organs of a real female, natal Saturn in the fifth house, ruling the marital seventh, shows the inability of the converted male to bear children. At forty-eight, Christine Jorgensen is still unmarried, since at one time the law refused to accept the former male as female and permit a legal marriage, which was then contemplated, and since in two other instances the engagement fell through.

There was, however, compensation, in a way, for the international publicity resulting from the change from male to female sex. After many years of little or no earning ability, the new surgically created female found that fame in the entertainment world could compensate for disadvantages in the commercial. From the time the conversion took place, financial rewards started to come from night-club appearances, the stage, and finally a popular autobiography giving all the hitherto withheld details of the sex change.

The chart shows how Neptune, in the house of earning ability, in close trine to Venus in the Mars-ruled sign Aries (in the house of reputation) brought this luck from the Mars-ruled operation. But Jupiter opposes Neptune in this chart, and the autobiography tells of several conflicts with the law because the police refused to accept the sex change as legitimate. Those who look for some occult explanation of why a man so completely female should live unwillingly as a male for most of his early life before realizing his desire to become a woman in physical form as well as nature, can look to the house of karmic credit, in which Jupiter is placed. This shows how service given to him at little cost made the conversion possible, and how luck or deserved good fortune made it possible through the trines between Pluto, Mars and Saturn in the natal chart.

An operation of this kind is fairly rare, however, and so likely to subject the individual to gossip and to wreck completely his personal reputation that more and more of these sexually maladjusted men and women are sentenced to social ostracism because of homosexual attitudes. Birth created them more heavily influenced by planets corresponding to a nature other than their physical sex, and if these planets rule houses in the chart which bring the individual in contact with the public, the result is tragic. Society does not tolerate obvious deviations from what is regarded as normal.

Yet few charts are so strongly masculine or feminine, because of the placement of most of the planets in one or the other type sign, that this division of qualities or inner nature cannot be found. Sometimes it takes only the ascendant-ruler and the position of the Moon to throw the

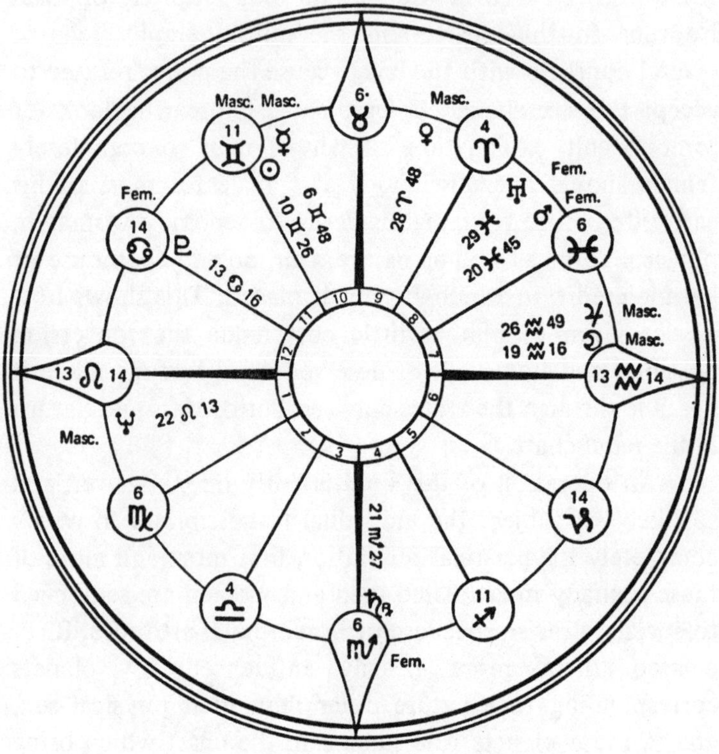

Marilyn Monroe
June 1, 1926, 9:30 am
Los Angeles, California

balance completely the opposite way from the actual sex. In the chart of the late Marilyn Monroe, a beautiful woman, all the same planets are in all the same signs in the birth chart as in Christine Jorgensen's chart, with the exception of the ascendant and the Moon, since Marilyn was born two days later in the same year in California. In Marilyn's chart, therefore, the Moon is in the male sign Aquarius and conjunct Jupiter in her seventh house to give her public approval and great popularity. The ascendant, Leo, is also a male sign and in the male decan ruled by Sagittarius. The problematic fixed cross, with Saturn in Scorpio, was therefore moved from the fifth house to the fourth, correlating with a Saturnian termination to the life, since it afflicted Neptune in Leo (close to the ascendant and ruling the eighth) and the Moon in Aquarius. Only two days' difference in date and a few hours' difference in time changed the course of this lovely girl's life from that which compelled a man to go to desperate lengths to be as feminine in appearance as his planets indicate he must have felt.

Many times the astrologer studies a seemingly normal personality and discovers feminine traits in a male and masculine attitudes in a female which the public never suspects. This is particularly true if the planets of the nature opposite to the sex of the client are in houses that give little contact with the world.

One such chart (First Example) shows a total of six planets and the ascendant in masculine signs, but four in feminine signs, creating a fine balance between the two potentials.

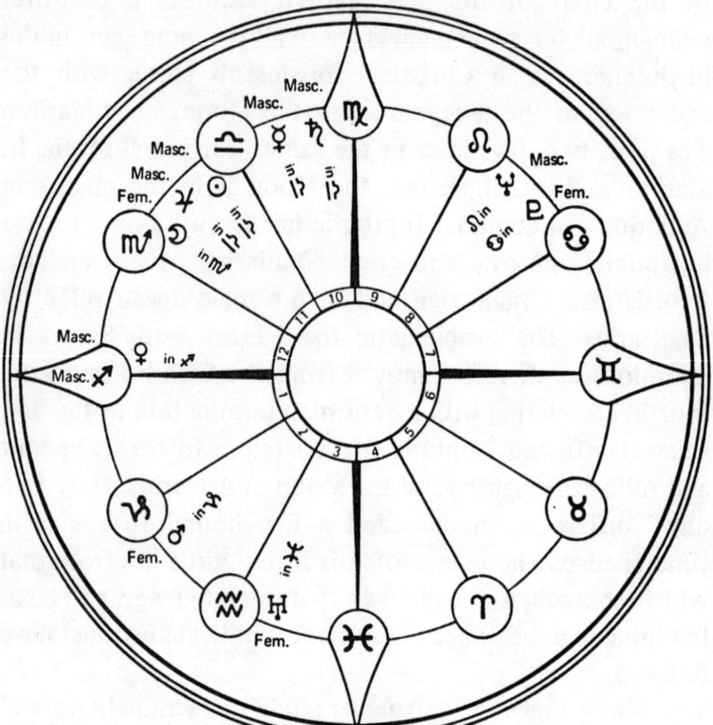

First Example
Man with six planets and the Ascendant
in masculine signs.

Fortunately the ruler of the ascendant is in a masculine sign and a masculine decan of that sign, so the appearance is definitely masculine. Venus is also in a male sign, as is Mercury, so only in those parts of the chart ruled by the feminine signs is any suggestion of feminine nature to be found. A feminine sign, however, rules the second house; therefore, the attitude toward material possessions and income is more like the typical woman's than the usually aggressive man's. A feminine sign rules the fourth cusp, and the gentle, negative, "good-wife" attitude is openly expressed in the home, supplementing, but never dominating, the interest of the wife in matters concerning the buying of food, and the care of the house and dependent members of the family.

A feminine sign rules the eleventh house, and this male prefers the friendship of any woman to male companionship, even though, in the sexual nature, Mars rules the fifth house.

Contrast this with the attitudes of a woman (Second Example) with six planets in feminine signs disposited by a male sign, and the ascendant and four planets in male signs. Since the Moon is in a feminine sign, the appearance is feminine, but with a male positive sign ruling the third house of the practical mind, the woman thinks like a man, speaks as men do, lacks interest in any feminine skills, preferring to do those things usually considered male duties or hobbies, and in every way concerning the third house is completely male. This masculine attitude is also expressed sexually, to the extent that there is no feminine attitude of submission in the sexual relationship, but

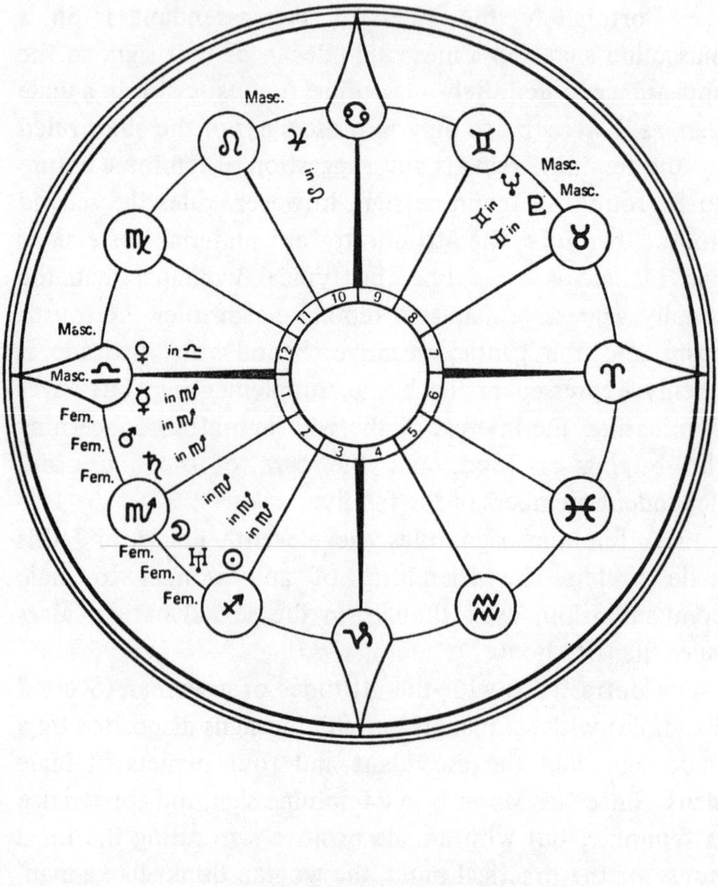

Second Example

Woman with six planets in feminine signs
but a masculine sign on the Ascendant.
Pluto, dispositor of all planets in Scorpio,
is in a masculine sign, giving balance.

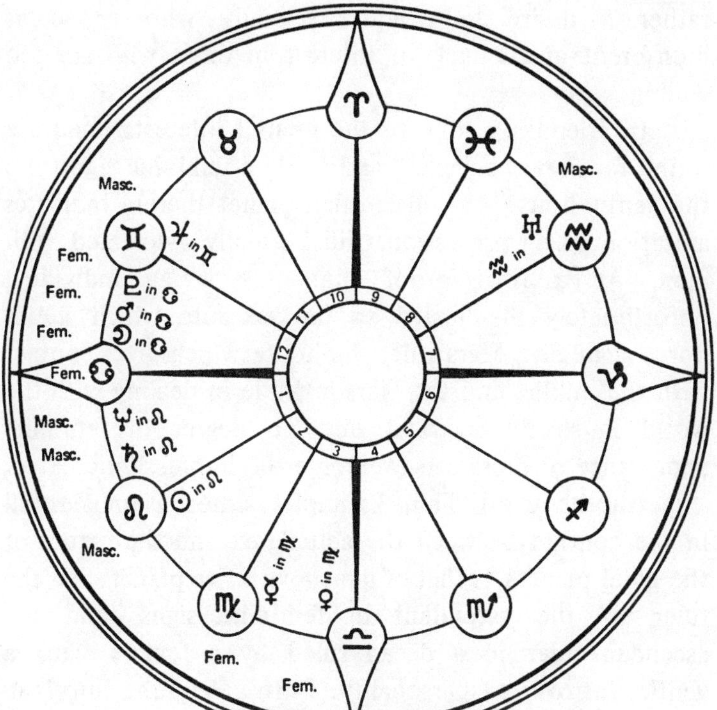

Third Example

Man with five planets and Ascendant in feminine signs.

rather a desire to conquer sexually whoever seems indifferent and a lack of interest in those who are too willing.

In friendship, due to the mental interests, men are found far more congenial, and while a feminine sign rules the tenth house, the male-ruled planet therein indicates ambition along professional lines usually associated with men. As a final proof that this is an individual unfortunately ill-adjusted to the sex into which she is born, aggressive Mars rules the house which gives contact with the public, and the Mars attitude in dealing with the world is so ill-concealed that no degree of feminine appearance or dress can overcome the impression created.

Another chart (Third Example), almost as unbalanced in the conflict between the actual sex and the nature of the natal planets, is that of a man with five planets and the ruler of the ascendant in feminine signs (and the ascendant-ruler in a decan ruled by a female sign)—a gentle, introverted personality. Fortunately the Sun is in the masculine sign Leo along with two other planets, and a fourth planet is in Aquarius. The fact that Neptune in Leo is close to the ascendant is of interest, suggesting an imitation of male personality rather than the type of man to be expected with three planets in a masculine sign like Leo. The mind is so feminine in its interests and attitudes that few women have more concern than he with the cleanliness of their house, the order of all rooms, the harmony of surroundings and the perfection of detail with which everything must be done. The ruler of the fourth house is Venus, and this orderly, perfectly operated but womanless home reveals the result of Libra's dispositor in the feminine sign Virgo, in conjunction to the natal Mercury in the third.

With Pluto, ruler of the fifth house, in the feminine sign Cancer, there is such a lack of interest in what we consider masculine sexual attitudes that we have no record of any sexual or romantic interests whatever in this life; yet this man is not homosexual, having no interest of any kind in men.

Saturn rules the seventh cusp and is in close conjunction to Neptune. The man has never married and seems to think that marriage should be a spiritual more than a physical relationship. Mars rules the important tenth house. Since it is in the most feminine of all signs and conjunct the Moon, the reputation undoubtedly suffers. Reflected here is what psychiatrists call an Oedipus complex, too close an attachment to the mother or a mother-substitute, as opposed to normal emotional attachments. A feminine sign rules the eleventh house: the best friends, and really the only friends, were women who, in a sense, were mother-substitutes. With the four Cancer planets in the karmic twelfth house, this is a chart weighted down with karmic debt to be discharged. Part of the punishment for past attitudes is the inability to adjust to what society thinks are normal personal relationships, yet the great concern with the good opinion of other men. In many ways, this chart presents almost the same kind of conflict of personality that is seen in the chart of Christine Jorgensen, but this individual tried to conform to what society expected of a man instead of seeking to surgically

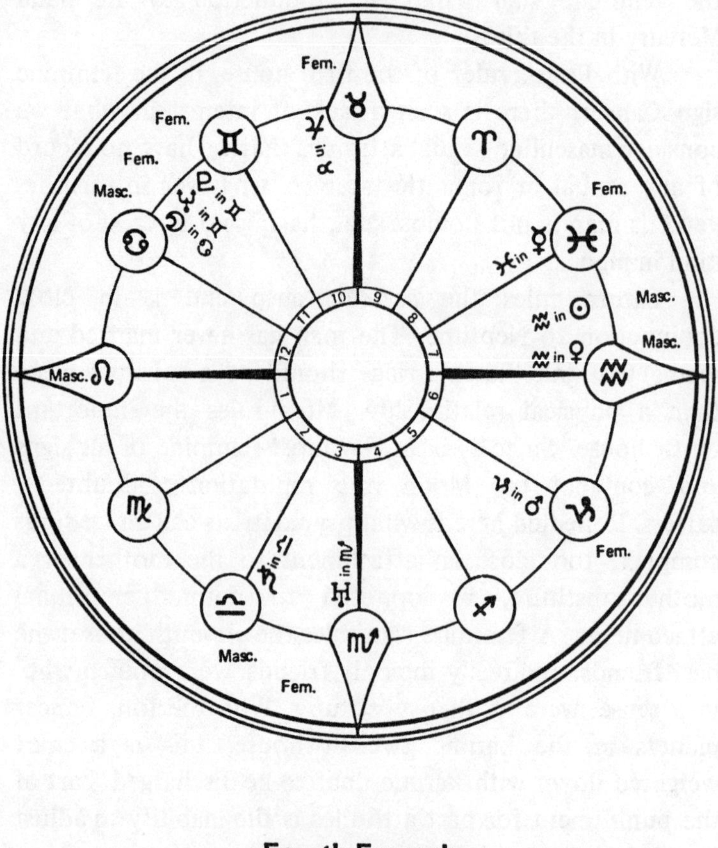

Fourth Example

Six planets in feminine signs

but four planets and the Ascendant in masculine signs.

match the physical self to the inner and mental nature.

The final example (Fourth Example) showing the delicate balance in male-female qualities is the chart of a man of mature years who has six planets in feminine signs, and four planets and the ascendant in masculine signs. Here is, from the ordinary viewpoint, a real man; yet the houses ruled by female signs show only such attitudes as are considered desirable or usual in women. Masculine Leo is on the ascendant, and this is a man who thinks that it is a man's world and that women are out of place except as wives, submissive and obedient to the male, and as mothers of children. The Sun and Venus are also in a masculine sign, as are the two planets in the seventh house, which Aquarius rules, so this all-male idea is most strongly expressed through marriage and in public contacts. The third house is also ruled by a sign of masculine nature, indicating only such interests as are suitable for men, in the opinion of other men. The sexual attitude is so definitely male that it is doubtful if this man could ever comprehend the female point of view in this relationship. But with so little ability to know a woman's needs, opinions and emotions, particularly in relation to those areas of life in which he is all man, he is in constant conflict with any woman in his life who is unwilling to be dominated. While such women are lucky for him (because there is a grand trine in this chart between the Moon, Uranus and Mercury), women often prove less than satisfactory as friends, and can deceive him, as indicated in a close square to Mercury in a female sign from Pluto and Neptune in a male sign, and in Mercury's placement in Neptune's sign.

Astrology thus shows why men and women are created of both male and female natures conjoined as the biblical words, "Male and female created he them," indicate. When a chart is so dominated by planets in signs of either nature that the individual cannot comprehend the attitudes of the opposite sex, difficulties of one kind or another are sure to result. Sometimes too many planets in signs of the same nature as the physical body, when there are too few in signs of an opposite nature, also produce imbalances and bring about problems in personal relationships, as in this male-dominant chart.

It is not enough to know the nature of each sign, whether masculine or feminine, and to let the preponderance determine the nature of the individual, whether positive or negative, masculine or feminine. It is also necessary to determine what planet disposits each sign-ruler under consideration, and what part of the chart those signs conflicting with the physical sex rule, since in some houses the characteristics of signs opposite the physical sex are scarcely noticed by the world. When they so dominate the personality's appearance and obvious attitudes, however, they can cause real social or personal problems.

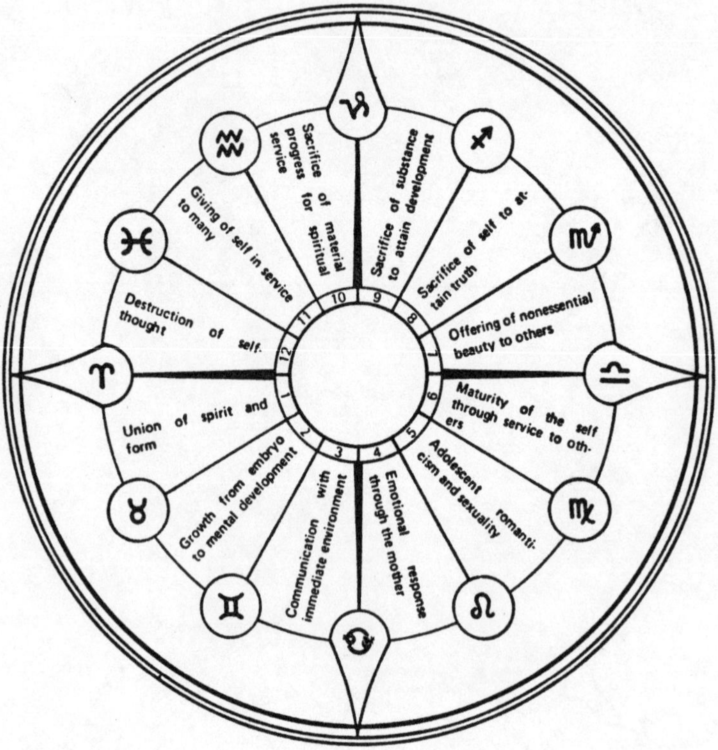

The Sequence of the Signs

5
The Sequence of the Signs

The sequence of the signs and therefore the order of the houses in a natural chart is not based on some arbitrary ruling offered by astrologers in earlier ages and accepted by all other practitioners of the art today. This natural order was determined by observation throughout centuries by those who combined awareness with reason as the source of knowledge.

This sequence may be seen as the result of conditions directly connected with human growth, as that growth from embryo to fullest maturity of body, mind and soul is the reflection of the growth of the cosmos.

Before man, as one of many monads cast forth from the Omnipotent Whole, descended by involution from non-form to physical life, life existed in what is described in the story of Genesis as "waters above and waters below"—the world of Neptune. We might say, therefore, that the true beginning of the zodiac is Pisces rather than Aries, since Pisces is the link between spirit and substance. Only after man, Adam, first of his species, was formed of the dust of the earth was the spirit housed in physical form.

In the cosmos, the source of all planets is the great central Sun, integrating spirit into cosmic substance.

Nothing which has life could commence growth if it were not fertilized; the fertilizing agent makes contact with the female part of plant, animal or human life, which corresponds to a receptive egg, in order to create new life.

Therefore, Pisces could be regarded as the original first sign in both the cosmos and other form, since it represents the union between spirit and substance in the creation of all universes. From it comes cosmic form, and union between substance and spirit creates all life.

Aries, symbolized by the horns of the ram from which life descends as spirit descends to impermeable substance, illustrates this union, which results in the birth of physical life and of form in cosmic space. Aries might be thought of as the first-born of spirit and substance—a complete form, aware in every way that it may exist independently of what gave it birth.

Since the birth chart is drawn for such forms or individuals or institutions which come into being on earth, the whole process of the development of mortal life reflects the continuous growth of the cosmos. The meaning of the phrase, "As above, so below," is clear, therefore, to those who think and observe. The macrocosm or grand man of the zodiac and the microcosm, man, are the symbols of the correspondence between two constitutions alike in function but tremendously different in scope.

One may illustrate this difference by saying that the atom in any whole structure could be considered the microcosm if compared to the macrocosm—the whole of which the atom is a minute part. Thus the sea might be likened to the macrocosm, and an atom of its spray might be considered the microcosm, since there is duplication of parts but vast difference in quantity. While the macrocosm, our universe, is far more magnificent than the microcosm of man, the macrocosm is not simply the enlarged reproduction of man but the very design from which mortal form was patterned.

Before earthly form existed, so-called life-form combined cosmic substance with vapor, as described in the book of Genesis, in a little understood chronicle of creation. The cosmos then might be compared to the state of the human embryo in its earliest stages before it shows form, although even at this stage it is a potential living creature.

♉ In the symbol which astrologers use for the sign Taurus, the nature of growth from embryo to mental development is shown, for Taurus is the complete circle of form surmounted by the curve of uplifted arms seeking to secure from the Source all material substance needed for life.

Earth, ruler of this earth sign, must seek from the source (the Sun) and from Neptune's vapor world the necessities for growing all that earth produces. Earth depends on Sun and water for its very functioning, as man, in the infant stage, depends upon food if he is to continue life. Without substance on which to feed, there can be no growth of any form of life, nor growth of cosmic form to greater dimension in space.

After life attains an adequate state of growth (which shows through the symbol of Taurus) by obtaining the necessities that are essential to physical well-being, the infant, when given strength and vitality to continue progress, comes to that point where the needs symbolized by the sign Gemini must be met. Gemini is an ideograph of the two arms with which the young child reaches out to grasp whatever is just beyond him in his immediate environment. The Mercury-ruled third house sign has to do with all forms of communication, short journeys, neighbors and the immediate vicinity. In the cosmos, this reaching out is communication between the various bodies in the universe, through electro-magnetic fields and gravity, and is made aware of such communication by the roar of the wind, the boom of thunder, the crackling of lightning—earthly analogs to communication in interplanetary space.

In the same way the infant reaches out to touch whatever is nearest and make sounds indicating desire, discomfort or satisfaction. Finding himself able to gain attention, the baby then reaches out or crawls toward the desired objects, and in time manages to step out and grasp what was otherwise beyond his reach. Thus he takes the first step in communication and travel and learns through contact with whatever is in close proximity. Our own earth is likewise seeking to reach out into cosmic space, through great space rockets, and make contact with other planetary bodies, so that earth-born man may learn the secrets of his environment in cosmic space.

It is possible to observe the progressive development of human life from the prenatal period to full maturity, and then to that point of disintegration man calls death. But since man cannot prove at this stage in science how the cosmos follows a similar pattern of growth and disintegration, why does he accept, as millions do, the teaching that he is created in a miniature mold duplicating the form of some superior Being? The answer may lie in his tremendous ego; he sees himself as the pattern and his Creator as reproducing his own form on a far more impressive scale of growth. He confuses the duplication of function with duplication of design, thus creating doubt where it is possible to observe truth.

After man finds that the necessities in life have been met, he finds that the emotional nature must also grow if he is to become mature. Emotional growth comes in the preadolescent, adolescent and postadolescent periods, during which sexual growth is also observable in changes of form, voice and personal attitudes.

♋ The first emotional response of the child is love for, and response to, the mother, or some substitute for her. Therefore, the fourth house and the fourth sign, which is Cancer, are ruled by the Moon, symbol of motherhood and maternal love. Maternal love is a self-giving Venus type of love which the growing child longs to know, but there is another role filled by the mother which is too often left to chance in the world today. Long after a child has learned to walk and talk and find many forms of self-expression, he is still in need of a maternal contact, since his development is not adequate for personal encounter with the outside world without this intermediary link.

In the cosmos the Moon is likewise the necessary intermediary between physical growth on the earth and the drastic, though necessary, action of the hot Sun. The light of the Moon, reflecting solar light softly, is known to supply all new, tender plant life with exactly the right impetus for growth during the hours when the Sun is not visible, conditioning it for the great heat of the noon Sun. Lack of this conditioning, like lack of maternal love and care, leaves form immature, lacking something more necessary for proper growth than is often realized. The immature plant as well as the young child need to develop in a protected way rather than be subjected to the drastic and rigorous disciplines of the Sun, the father, or the world of adult life.

The Sun, like male energy and force, is too rigid, tco extreme, to deal with early growth in nature as is a human father to deal with the early emotional growth of the child. The highly sensitive child grows best under the influence of the mother, in the same way that the sensitive tendrils of the plant put forth better growth under the reflected light given by the Moon. Even in nature it is necessary to temper the Sun's light with artificial shade if some fragile and delicate plants are not to burn or wither under what, to others, is life-giving energy.

In the first seven years of life, the child must know the shielding qualities of maternal love if he is not to be distorted and wrongly conditioned by direct contact with formidable and wrongly conditioned by direct contact with formidable male thought. He will, of course, come to know a certain amount of this, since maternal thought is usually a reflection of parental, tempered to meet the conditions of the immature soul.

When we come to the next sign, Leo, the natural ruler of the fifth house, ruled by the Sun, the first quality of adolescent, romantic thought manifests, as well as creative ideas and the development of the sexual nature as the result of desire or romantic love. Through the nature of this sign, and those things which it rules, the adolescent human comes to awareness of self, or form, of soul. Through the quality of preadolescent thought there comes a realization of the qualities of the self as alien to other forms and this awareness demands expression in relation to others. In the same manner, the Sun shines through clouds to express its own nature and, like the adolescent youth, to impress its quality upon the world in a continuous effort at self-expression.

Following the emotional growth seen in the fifth house sign, there comes another necessary manner of growth seldom welcome and often little understood as contributing to complete maturity. The sixth house, natural house of Virgo, is ruled by Vulcan, and since it is Vulcan of all the gods who gave service, this house has always been called a house of service, differentiated from the tenth, where man expresses his personality, for only in service to others may a man develop and lift his soul to higher levels. Through service he comes to maturity and learns by doing many things not taught in the primary education that was another facet of fifth house development.

Without service to the world or to others, the soul learns less of truth and the self lives with only thoughts of itself.

When man comes to the point where he is willing to do what is required by others, he is ready to enter a relationship which, for full expression, demands service to another before service to himself. In the seventh house sign, Libra, ruled by Venus, there must be concern for the welfare of another rather than concentration on the satisfactions of the self. Thus man reaches full maturity in this seventh house experience.

After all fundamental needs for growth and functioning have been met, the cosmos comes to the point where, instead of serving only its own needs, it begins to offer to other cosmic forms those things which might be considered nonessential, since life may exist without them.

Following the same thought, a man may live without marriage; lacking this experience, however, or any form of partnership in which another must be considered, he misses one of the experiences of growth, for at this stage of development he might desire to share with another whatever gives luxury, beauty, pleasure or profit to him.

The cosmos also develops to the point where it creates beauty above and beyond necessity, so freely and in such full measure that it provides for all a service of love, bringing beauty to the earth through floral colors, the brilliant plumage of the birds, the hues of sunrise and sunset—all attributes of Venus. These are not necessary for functioning, but are gifts from the cosmos to created life. For this same reason, man finds many things lovelier when he comes to a willingness to share whatever beauty he may create with others.

Libra is the point of balance (symbolized by the balance itself) between the self and the spirit or not-self, whether balance is attained through sharing with another in marriage or the partnership between the cosmos and mortal form, in which cosmic energy gives forth solar radiations, stimulating and maintaining life by supplying necessary substance.

From this midpoint in growth, the self, too, comes to express more selfless interests, since nothing more is required for physical growth or material gain. Much more, however, is needed for spiritual development and for greater awareness of the self through the expansion and progress of the soul housed in that self.

It might be said that as man evolves from the earliest sign of finite life, Aries, through the lower segment of the successive houses, he is developing through a series of personal lessons gained through finite experience. When at last he reaches Libra, the first demand for thought of others is made, and in each sign above the point of balance, the progress of the soul results from impersonal and unselfish desire for further growth.

Scorpio, ruled by a little understood planet, Pluto, is the sign in which material form willingly sacrifices some part of its quantity of growth or destroys substance so that it may attain quality of development. Unless the personal attitudes are destroyed, neither Scorpio nor any other sign can develop beyond personal and limited self-expression.

Through its Pluto rulership Scorpio is far more involved in the growth of all forms of life than any other sign, since it rules sexual functioning and therefore is a necessary part of all life. But the individual Scorpio sees only the necessity of self-expression and self-satisfaction until, through voluntary and drastic disciplines, he attains the qualities of the higher self by destroying any defects of the personality. By doing this, he reaches a state of progress at which, like the legendary phoenix, he may wing his way into realms of spirit and come to awareness of all truth, all intelligence, all of the Omnipotent Whole.

This is Scorpio's quest for selflessness, its desire to conquer self-will that it may do the will of the Highest Form. Scorpio's ruler, Pluto, is Lucifer, the fallen angel, the sexual power in man through which he can create life, but fallen to the basest level through gratification of the self.

Scorpio destroys itself in interludes of self-gratification, but when the time comes for man to seek truth, it is Scorpio who says, "I have found so little of worth in physical life that I would learn whatever is worth in the Highest Form." It is the man or woman who has descended to the very sewers of life in past eons of living who first finds life of little worth. But when Scorpio desires more than can be found in mortal life, that desire can be satisfied only through oneness with spiritual truth.

Sagittarius, the ninth house sign, makes a sacrifice of material substance rather than of self-satisfactions. The quality of Jupiter, ruler of this sign, reflects itself in unselfish thought for others demonstrated by giving substance and making material offering to benefit the less fortunate. This Sagittarius can easily do, for this sign grows through the increase of substance given by the Source to all those who give freely of what is theirs to others.

The sacrifice which Capricorn, the tenth house sign, must make is a kind of giving more difficult for a Saturn-ruled personality than any other. Saturn is the biblical Satan, tempter of Christ's soul. Satan may seem oddly unfit to rule a sign of spiritual progress unless one understands that when the Master Jesus was taken to a high mountain, and there offered the kingdoms of the earth in exchange for spiritual rewards, temptation was put before One who had already come to know the greatest spiritual progress. Thus He was better able to reject what might to others seem the highest reward—all that earth offers—since only those who have come to know truth can compare its value with finite treasures. By progressive growth through successive signs, natives of Capricorn must come to this tenth house pinnacle after knowing life in the period of Sagittarius soul-growth that gives great truth from the Source. In the Capricorn incarnations, only growth in material ways seems important, and when this has been accomplished, sacrifice of what is almost Capricorn's life-blood is more difficult for a Capricorn than for other signs. A man who has sacrificed his soul for material profit does not find it easy to renounce such gain in the desire to serve God in selfless but unprofitable work.

Sagittarius sacrifices substance, of which he has plenty. Scorpio sacrifices himself or his life, finding neither really satisfactory, to gain truth. Capricorn must sacrifice what was most vitally required for his self-satisfaction to rise to spiritual heights. Hence those who reject the kingdoms of the world for spiritual service must make the greatest sacrifice.

In Aquarius the student finds the antithesis of Leo's attitude of self-expression. Aquarius seeks to express the not-self through the giving of himself in service to many. Not only is the Aquarian willing to put his own ego aside so that another may profit from what he desires, but when he is truly beneficent he becomes so humble that there are none who do not seem to him soul-brothers. In thought, the evolved Aquarian seeks to build, side by side with his own soul's development, the spiritual quality of many souls, so that they may become identical with him in all qualities. See how the symbol of Aquarius shows a succession of little tent-like lines side by side, none lifted higher than any other in prestige or progress toward good.

What astrologers now consider the final sign, Pisces, shows how the soul desires to destroy all thoughts of self, so that it may become a part of the Omnipotent Whole and in time be free of the necessity of earth experience.

In each of the signs man's immortal soul learns some fundamental lesson: first, through personal experience; then through impersonal attitudes in which each soul makes sacrifices in some form for the good of others so that it may become a part of the Source from which all souls first came, and to which, in many periods of time, all hope to return.

6
Man and His Money

When the hour of birth is exactly known, there are astrological rules which can throw much light on any matter. When the time of birth is unknown, the most satisfactory plan is to draw the solar chart, putting the Sun's degree on the date of birth on the ascendant, and the same degree of each succeeding sign on each house cusp.

This will reveal the way the soul or etheric form feels, for example, in relation to all matters of income and material possessions. Since the emotional pattern conditioned by the soul determines in a large measure what the individual is to become, this method of constructing the chart will show much which could not otherwise be known in advance.

The man or woman with the *Sun in Aries,* while inclined to rush into new adventures, can accumulate material possessions and show a very practical attitude toward money, since Taurus is the natural ruler of the money house of this sign. But Taurus is ruled by the practical earth and for Aries the earth is in its opposite sign, Venus-ruled Libra, for the position of the earth in any chart is always directly opposite the Sun by sign and equal in degree. Thus, while Aries earns and enjoys earning and piling up income, he often spends for luxury.

With the *Sun in Taurus* on the first cusp, Gemini will be the ruler of the second house, indicating a mental attitude in relation to money. It shows the nature of Taurus to desire two sources of income. The dual nature of Gemini fits perfectly into the Taurean desire not to gain all his income from one source, but to have another fairly secure one to fall back on in case he runs short.

The solar chart is the soul chart. In other words, it shows the nature of the inner self, the etheric desire nature, the motive power that stimulates the self, all expressed through the Sun.

The Sun in Taurus is in an earth sign. It has fixed form; therefore, it does the things it desires to do, rather than merely speaking or thinking of them. It is also the natural second house sign, so its "soul" purpose is to act to bring results along lines of material possessions, earning ability, and the accumulation of such things that prove the Taurean has the power to add to what he wants through the dual efforts of the Gemini solar second house. But Gemini is a Mercury sign; Mercury is the practical mind; therefore, the Taurus does not desire to work merely for cash. He wants to work for whatever the world conceives of as wealth. He wants to be known by the community as "wealthy," not merely to have money. He is more inclined than any of the other twelve signs to put emphasis on what money buys. He is willing to work for what he gets, to work along two lines in order to get as much as possible or as he thinks needful and important. But he wants the whole world to know that he has money and that he has the ability to gain through the mental attitude of Gemini.

Although Taurus is an earth sign, the Taurean is not by choice the laborer. The Taurean chooses to work with the mind along practical lines. He sells, travels, writes, and in a sense thinks constantly of ways to add to his income, to increase the material possessions that can be gained through intelligent ideas.

The man or woman who has the *Sun in Gemini* has another attitude toward income. The ever-changing Moon, ruler of Cancer, is the natural ruler of Gemini's second house. Therefore, the income of one with the Sun in Gemini frequently fluctuates. Those who write, or travel, or who do the mental types of work characteristic of Gemini frequently do not have stable incomes. The nature of Cancer is subject to the ebb and flow of the tides of the ocean. There is increase and decrease. There is a joining together of two sources to create one. The typical Gemini's idea for material profit is to work with two aptitudes in order to adequately supply himself with the material things he wants.

He frequently does this. He does not put all his eggs in one basket, but has, if it is needed, another basket handy to carry any bacon he may get. Many times, however, he must put whatever he gains in both baskets to provide a full meal! The Gemini is not the best income-producer, as far as security of income goes, because he is lacking in the steadfastness of pursuit of wealth characteristic of Taurus. He is not devoted to the business of getting rich, but interested in practical experience and in moving here, there, and everywhere in order to get it. Like the rolling stone that gathers no moss, Gemini is too restless, too unwilling to stick to one thing, too lacking in the power of concentration to get all that he could through the mental activity of which he is capable. He produces only what he needs, and in the way Cancer indicates—in periods of ebb and flow, coming and going. Sometimes he is well off, at other times he just manages to get by, but often he is without the satisfaction of having an income always adequate to meet all needs.

According to the nature of each sign, with the solar chart the astrologer may see the soul's attitude toward every department in the life, as may be realized when the natural ruler of each house in a chart is studied.

Because of the dominant interest of the person with *Sun in Cancer* in his children, most of his financial problems center on the sign naturally ruling the fifth house and his solar second—children, education and sometimes entertainment. This often includes the family to which he is frequently tightly bound.

The Cancerian is somewhat inclined to hold on to little amounts to the point of being called penny-pinching. But when it comes to purchasing things which will add to the pleasure of his family or make them more comfortable or better able to maintain their rightful position, he lets larger amounts go freely. Spending for the children's schooling, for travel for the whole family, for pleasure in which all children share, he willingly does, but in other ways he watches the pennies.

Since Leo is his money house sign and is ruled by the Sun and definitely centered in itself, the Cancerian is less likely to put income or outgo on a wider scale than the domestic. And though he does not scrimp with his family, neither does he waste. The Cancer's tendency is to hold onto old furnishings, old clothing, and whatever belongs to the past, so he does not spend for other than the necessities which go to make up the comfortable home.

Regal *Sun in Leo* likes to spend for services. What Leo was ever willing to eat in a restaurant which requires the customer to carry his own tray? The cost of service to him is just as important and essential as the cost of food, and this includes service in every field in which it is available. He wants it as perfect and as meticulous as Virgo, his second house sign, can give. Nothing but the best suits him. In spite of the thought that the typical Leo is given to free spending, actually he expects more for what he spends than most signs. His real generosity lies in his willingness to pay well when he is flattered and satisfactorily served, his always-important ego remaining untarnished by any shabby treatment.

Should Leo find it essential to serve in some capacity himself, however, he serves as Vulcan, the ruler of Virgo did—as a real member of the Olympian circle descending to mortal form to assist the human race and gain their admiration for what he can do by the perfection of his own production. Acting is typical of the kind of service the Leo is willing to give to the world–personal but demanding of acclaim as well as financial reward. Leo, outside the entertainment world, prefers the executive position which gives personal recognition. Money to him is less important than prestige, but authority in his own field is practically essential for his contentment.

Whereas Leo demands perfection in the service he gets from others, the individual with *Sun in Virgo* looks for perfection in everything. Such superior quality of workmanship costs more than the cheap or ordinary; thus Virgo spends for quality and fine workmanship. By giving superior service himself, he often finds it easy to earn and pleasant to serve. Since Venus rules Libra in the solar house of income, he purchases clothing that speaks of luxury, good taste and detail, and that costs above average. Since Virgo is the most practical of all signs, however, he wastes nothing. He buys what endures, remains in style for a long time, and gives pleasure to others as well as to the purchaser. He wastes nothing on poor materials or inferior equipment. Money to him is somewhat of a source of pleasure, since it provides him with the things most necessary for his comfort and complete satisfaction. Whatever spending Virgo does, however, is to satisfy his own requirements, seldom the desires of another.

With *Sun in Libra* the native seldom feels the waste of money through self-indulgence, even though his income is limited, since Scorpio, ruling Libra's money house, is sign-ruler of the house of partnership income. The feminine Libran who must spend her own money for the luxuries she considers as necessary is rare. There is always someone, particularly a husband, willing to spend on a woman looking as lovely as only Libra can. Because Libra spends for luxury rather than service in what he or she buys, however, what is spent is often wasted or rejected as outdated after a few months use. Hence the sign does not accumulate money other than what comes through partnership or marriage with more practical types. Saving money at the cost of inconvenience or scrimping is something Libra does not do. The average woman and many men born in this sign see money as necessary only for what can be bought to give a momentary pleasure to them and to those with whom they are always willing to share what they have.

When the *Sun is in Scorpio,* Sagittarius, ruled by expansive Jupiter, is on the cusp of the second house. It is no accident that several of the world's greatest fortunes are in the hands of Scorpio women through eighth house inheritance or, as the case of former Hetty Green, amazing luck in speculation; all because Jupiter, ruler of Sagittarius, is the planet of growth, expansion, and increase, and in the mental sign. As a result, the Scorpio individual thinks in terms of constantly increasing income and material substance, and of making his store of worldly goods bigger and even bigger, never ceasing until he can show the whole world that Scorpio seizes upon the smallest opportunities and sometimes, in a single lifetime, produces the greatest possible income. It is the nature of Scorpio to see no reason to limit what is the ever-expanding Sagittarius-Jupiter quality of that second house.

There is a great difference in the second house nature of the person with *Sun in Sagittarius.* Strangely enough, Capricorn on the cusp of this second house makes the most conservative of all spenders. A man who seems less fortunate than many might always be in search of a so-called lucky break, but the man who is well provided for sees as the first necessity the need of protecting what he already has. Therefore, the Sagittarius with great wealth is the world's most conservative spender and, in a sense, the accumulator of the fixed and solid possessions and investments available to great wealth. More men who are monied put money back into preferred stocks, and guaranteed first mortgages, government bonds, and make conservative, nonspeculative use of that with which they are provided than any once-penniless pauper ever thinks of doing. The nature of Saturn is expressed through the second house of Sagittarius. Saturn rules the ultraconservative and is not indicative of speculation in any sense of the word. Sagittarians show the true caution of Saturn in the way they protect what they make, what they inherit, and what they have the luck to acquire.

More than this, they regard money itself as a great responsibility; therefore the caution of Saturn is often expressed through inheritance, which serves to protect what they have already amassed. A wealthy Sagittarian who is profligate with what he has is likely to have a chart afflicted by the planetary ruler of his Sagittarius ascendant, Jupiter; but in general the wealthy Sagittarian is conservative.

On the other hand, there is something of a quality of chance in the nature of Aquarius, the second house ruler of the person with *Sun in Capricorn.* True, he is preeminently a long-range planner. He makes, from the very early years, an effort to attain the highest possible position, particularly in the business world. But if he is poor at birth, as often happens, he has the strength of Saturn to climb from lowly beginnings to great attainment. He knows what it is to be without, particularly without wealth, so he is less concerned than other men about money. He has been poor, but having climbed from poverty to high position, he knows that if he puts forth the same effort he may regain whatever he might lose. He is willing, therefore, to take a chance.

This is Capricorn's true nature. He does exactly what the goat does—climbs the rocky crags to reach the highest point, but takes more chances in doing so than any sheep grazing in the level meadow. If the goat is not provided with good grazing land by difficult and risky climbing, he goes after a place where he may secure adequate food. Capricorn does this in gaining the preeminence of position that eventually belongs to him. He often earns in a way which can well be described by Aquarius on the cusp of the second house of his solar chart.

He pits his own capabilities against chance, with the

idea, "If I win, I'll gain what is a sudden fortune, but if I fall back I can always regain what I have lost, because I know that I am capable of climbing to the top again." Thus in spite of the conservative nature of one with Sun in Capricorn, there is less caution in relation to the things of the second house than a Saturnian nature might be expected to show.

Aquarius on the second cusp brings income from unusual sources, in unexpected ways, and sometimes gives a rather odd and out-of-the-ordinary way of earning. Those who think the Capricorn is not the Aquarian in the way he handles his money, even though he takes a chance, should check the number of Capricorn financiers and find how few there are who fail to speculate on the wildest possible schemes. Let them see the opportunity for big profit by climbing high, and they climb, no matter how dangerous and steep the trail may be. Therefore, Uranus ruling the solar second cusp of Capricorn indicates the out-of-the-ordinary attitude toward both earning power and material possessions.

Frequently Capricorn buys for personal use true oddities which are not only extraordinary in their nature, but unusual to the extent that they are actually curiosities.

The philosophical person with *Sun in Aquarius,* with impractical Pisces ruling his monetary house, has a similar way of making money or paying bills, since Neptune, Pisces' ruler, is the planet least concerned with material problems. The Aquarian thinks of life in terms of human relationships rather than financial responsibilities, and puts friendship above what it costs to be a friend.

Since Pisces as financial ruler will make the concept of earning a living rather impractical, the Aquarian often goes into some field of work where the chance for earning is limited and the profits almost nonexistent. In payment of what he owes others he is, alas, likely to think that they, too, think this same way and to overlook payment of bills until they are long past due. His friends, it may be thought, appreciate his willingness to wait indefinitely for loans to be repaid more than his creditors appreciate his indifference to meeting payment dates.

The person with *Sun in Pisces,* being a Neptunian type himself, lacks concern about saving money and spends enthusiastically, as might be expected with Aries ruling his solar second cusp. He buys, when he has money to do so, as recklessly and carelessly as Virgo spends cautiously and thriftily. In addition, he spends wastefully, buying without practical advance planning. Often the money he earns is of less benefit to him than money is to other signs because of this lack of foresight, but he has always the adventurous hope that in some new and usually impractical enterprise he may earn more.

Regardless of what sign may be on the cusp of the second house in a chart drawn for a specific time of birth, much additional information regarding the way the individual earns, spends and thinks of money may be gained if the natural ruler of the sign on the cusp of the second solar house is also considered. In many cases, this sort of analysis also shows the way possessions will be accumulated and their nature.

7
Lessons of Marriage

For an analysis of the effects of marriage on the individual, the student should consider both the natal chart, if the correct time of birth is known, and the solar chart.

The seventh house shows the condition in marriage so far as it affects the individual, and the problems or benefits which will result from the marriage. Even in this era of multiple marriages, the seventh house remains the key, though conditions may be tempered or intensified by the nature of the second or third partner in relation to that of the individual, since marriage is always a relationship through which experience must be gained.

The position of the Sun by sign, however, and also the quality of the sign in which it may be, is basically important, for these show the nature of the lessons that the individual incarnated in the present life must learn.

Fixed Signs

The four fixed signs express attitudes through what they do or dislike to do. Thus Taurus is much interested in income; Leo, in his children as expressions of his own ego; Scorpio, with sexual problems or transmutation of sexual into occult power (and on the material level with the handling of shared income); and Aquarius, with relationships to friends.

Should the natal Sun be in *Taurus,* regardless of the house it occupies, the person is incarnated to gain experience in handling, earning or constructively using income and material possessions. The Taurean will find himself concerned with money problems–learning how to content himself with too little or manage wisely all he can accumulate.

Though *Leo* is associated in the popular mind with romance, the Leo man or woman after marriage is more concerned with the children resulting from the marriage than with the marriage partner. Leo desires to reproduce himself in his offspring. His love for them and his desire to shape their lives is really the expression of his own self-love or desire to accomplish through them something he failed to do himself. In the somewhat rare marriages in which there are no children, the Leo male still sees himself as so self-sufficient that he wants neither advice nor assistance from the marriage partner. He demands complete and undisputed rule over the destiny of the family and home and control of all finances. While he is generous to those who ask of his bounty, he regards it as *his* privilege to offer it–not *their* right to share. This, to those who regard marriage as a mutual benefit association, is cause for more discontent and resentment than can be compensated for by Leo's generous favors.

If the Sun is in *Scorpio,* lessons of sexual relationship are a part of the soul's development, and the importance of lifting the power of sex to a level more vitally important than the physical has to be learned, as well as constructive attitudes in relation to the income of legal or marital partnership. Malefic planets ruling the seventh house in a birth or solar chart suggest that these matters will be problems in marriage.

To the *Aquarian,* friends are of the utmost importance and the effect they have on his life, either for good or ill, is far greater than can be realized. Because Aquarius is the highest development among the fixed signs, the Aquarian gives of himself in friendship and impersonal concern for the less privileged, but the lack of personal feeling expressed in his attitude often leaves doubt in the mind of the recipient that any feeling exists. This can and often does create discord in personal relationships. The sign Aquarius is directly opposed to Leo and its ego, and in even greater conflict with the intensely personal and emotional nature of Scorpio, which demands all or nothing in intimate relationships. Through all the fixed signs, however, the nature of the Sun must be expressed through positive or negative attitudes. These signs must do something to learn lessons that can only be understood by the functioning of the self.

Mutable Signs

With the mutable (mental) signs, mental contacts create new concepts through stimulation from, and association with, other minds in intimate relationship.

The Sun in *Gemini* at birth creates problems in relation to brothers and sisters, immediate neighbors, letters and other communications, and indicates desire for more travel than other signs find important. Because Gemini is a mental sign, the problem may consist more in a mental attitude than in the material conditions. The Gemini may worry about those conditions, but sometimes does little more than protest.

In marriage, the *Virgo* partner serves, as Virgo does in all relationships of life, so the selfish or self-centered partner in such a marriage is very well served in every way. But there is such lack of romance, such emphasis on duty and routine and perfection in even the least important matters, that such a relationship is better for business than romance. Marriage for a Virgo is the test of his responsibility to follow routine duties, and accept the conditions imposed upon him. But he expects that this same attention to system and detail will be given by the partner, who may lack such virtues, so marriage to a Virgo may be more than imperfect mortals can accept.

Sagittarius shows almost the opposite idea of what marriage should be. This Jupiter-ruled sign is free spending, but also demanding of more personal freedom both before and after marriage than any sign other than Libra. Sagittarius is so lacking in sexual warmth that some women would feel unwanted in spite of the partner's generosity in material things. Women of the opposite nature might also resent the Sagittarian attraction to unrestricted, long vacations to distant lands, overexpansive ideas and too-free spending. The Sagittarian needs to learn restraint of personal freedom or overexpansion when married to someone who cannot understand his typically Jupiterian attitudes.

Somewhat the same submissive and masochistic mental attitude which makes Virgo serve without complaint is characteristic of the *Piscean,* who seems to delight in ill-treatment from others. Unless this solar type has some reason to feel imposed upon or unappreciated, he seems to lack reason for living. While some Piscean wives or husbands often are abused and ill-used by a more dominant partner (since it is human nature to impose upon those who permit imposition), the extreme to which many of these individuals go can only be understood if it is realized that the Sun in this sign is completing a final cycle of incarnation: the soul is unknowingly seeking to expiate any sins of past lives. This is the logical reason why the natural Pisces twelfth house is sometimes called the "house of self-undoing." The soul incarnated in this sign truly seeks to undo whatever the self may have done in this or past lives, so that it may feel completely exonerated. Therefore, it does as much as is possible to destroy whatever remains of self-interest, self-desire, and selfishness by permitting and often inviting imposition from others. This, of course, is really injustice to the spouse, since it tends to encourage unfairness that might not have come about had it been opposed. But for the partner in marriage who insists upon domination, the Piscean is a problem chiefly because of his lack of practical attitudes and his indifference to creating financial security for himself and others.

Cardinal Signs

When the Sun is in a cardinal sign, the inner self is expressed very clearly through the personality, since the cardinal signs reveal the motivating nature.

With the Sun in *Aries,* the soul expresses, as does the child through great activity, reckless courage and new ventures of a kind which would not be undertaken by more practical natures.

The Sun in *Cancer* offers only the limited field of the fourth house to gain self-expression, but here the maternal and protective nature finds the best opportunity to function and the Cancerian gains great control over the self. Although Cancer is ruled by the Moon and, as a water sign, is not compatible with the nature of the Sun, within his own limitations the Cancerian will express himself through all fourth house matters and find the conditions this house rules most congenial and harmonious.

Libra's lesson, however, must always be in connection with partnership and marriage. Therefore, some astrologers insist that the true Libran marries early and often. He feels the need of close association with a partner more than other signs do, yet because Libra is an air sign, he seeks to be as free as the air, and this is only possible when no bonds interfere with such freedom.

Libra is the sign which marks the turning point between the lower six signs, which learn through experiences of a strictly personal nature or without need of association with another, and the six signs that teach through association with others or through impersonal relationships. The Libran returns to incarnation to learn to live contentedly in partnership. This requires both the peace-loving and harmonious nature of this sign and considerably more energy and continued effort than any true Libran shows.

In a partnership with a sign of opposite nature, the Libran must surrender much of the personal freedom he desires or find marriage less serene than he prefers. In view of this sign's dislike of drudgery, the partner in marriage or in business must carry the burden, and this often creates disharmony. Only when both partners do not have to cope with the practical problems of paychecks and labor that demands sweat and determination, is it possible for marriage to be the sort Libra seeks. So the usual problem in marriage for this sign is: who does the work while the Libran promotes the beauty and harmony of life? When the husband is a Libran, this creates a situation usually not conducive to prolonged harmony. Where the Libran is the wife, marriage may prove more successful if—and only if—the husband can look upon the lovely woman of his choice as a luxury he can afford for the pleasure she gives, and charge her off on his income tax as the financial liability she is likely to be.

Capricorn, the last of the cardinal signs, is of the earth element and therefore expresses its nature in material ways through ambition and professional growth. This permits the Capricorn to make far-sighted plans and express ambition-promoted ideas that may result in more than ordinary power on the material level. Yet this can mitigate against the Capricorn's family relationships in marriage and the home, for the man who succeeds often must sacrifice much of his personal life for professional accomplishment. The problem of the Capricorn in marriage is to find a balance between ambition for public success and consideration for those who depend upon him for companionship and happiness. The Capricorn man or woman may find a rewarding career preferable to love on little income, and social position of greater importance than the role of husband or housewife.

For every soul there is some obvious reason for reincarnation, some lesson which must be learned through this present life experience, often at considerable cost or sacrifice. Much of what seems illogical and unreasonable is shown to be completely necessary if this is realized. The personal chart shows not only why the soul returned again for necessary earthly lessons, but the manner in which such lessons will be learned.

Yet, as in every college, there may be opportunities to avoid what is offered and choose only a course that appeals to the desire of all men to do what can be done with the least effort. But there is no substitute for experience if the soul has come to the point of truth which releases it from the need of further incarnations. What one needs to learn through the interpretation of the birth chart is not what to avoid so that life is less difficult, but what to accept to qualify for final promotion to a higher realm of truth. Man does not come into mortal life to make pleasant situations for himself, but to find the best way to turn an unpleasant situation into a profitable or truth-revealing experience.

It is not intelligent, for this reason, to consider some aspects in a natal chart as unfortunate and others as lucky because the latter give reward for little effort in some department of life. The so-called unfortunate aspects are the lessons required for the complete education of the soul. The lucky aspects in the natal chart show that in connection with certain matters in the individual's life, he has been given credit for previous lessons well learned or for good thoughts of others.

In marriage, a lesson most mortals must learn, the need is to offer the best qualities of one's Sun-sign in order to create a partnership in which both individuals share benefits equally and contribute constructively the qualities most needed to supplement what may be lacking in the nature of the other partner. This is, of course, not the popular concept of marriage in America—hence perhaps the failure and dissolution of so many marriages. Those who seek freedom through divorce are drop-outs in the school of life experience, but in some future incarnation they must re-enroll and complete the course, if soul-progress is to be made.

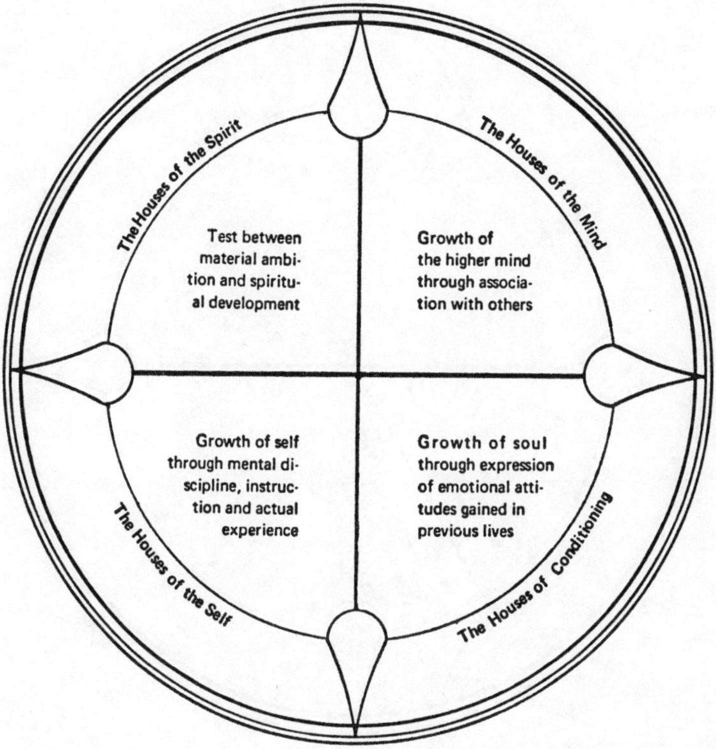
The Houses of the Spirit
The Houses of the Mind
The Houses of the Self
The Houses of Conditioning
Test between material ambition and spiritual development
Growth of the higher mind through association with others
Growth of self through mental discipline, instruction and actual experience
Growth of soul through expression of emotional attitudes gained in previous lives

Man's Fourfold Nature

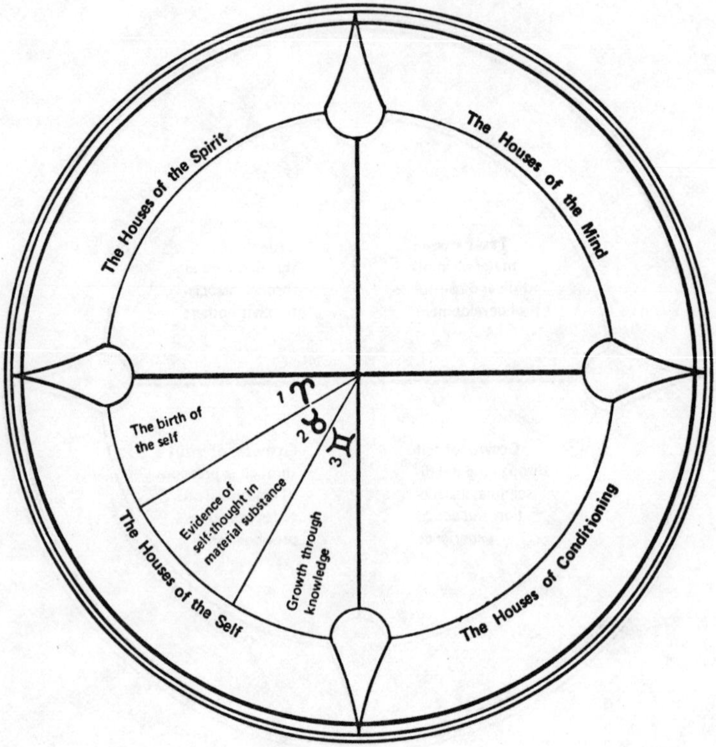

The Houses of the Self

8
The Houses of the Self

In interpreting the meaning of each sign and natural house in any chart, the student must know the nature of the ruler of the sign on the cusp of the house, and through this the nature of that house.

Since, for example, Mars rules the sign Aries, those who are fully familiar with the nature of Mars know the qualities of Aries. Those born with Aries on the ascendant partake of the characteristics of Mars; they act according to the nature of Mars, and show the attitude of Mars in all they do, think and say.

If Mars is on the ascendant, or rules the first house, it indicates a Mars type of personality: aggressive, energetic, adventurous, given to the exploration of new places and ideas, and inclined to make fast starts along new lines of activity. Therefore, the Mars-type, or one with this planet in the first house, gives impetus to thought, feeling and action.

This type, as a result of such tendencies, is inclined to clash with whatever, or whomever, opposes his will, and to rush ahead without preparatory work, even though caution might solidify and secure his position.

First House: Aries

The first house, or the natural house of *Aries*, represents the self, and only the self. It stands for the appearance, the manner, the quality, and the quantity of the self—the personality which identifies the individual.

By analysis of the ascendant, or first house qualities, the astrologer can form an opinion of any person. It is most important to know what the qualities of the whole personality are. If, in the chart, there are indications that other planets indicate tendencies of an entirely different nature, it is evident that the appearance and manner may serve as a disguise. The appearance may be simply a front, hiding qualities of a very different nature than those indicated on the first contact.

With Mars in or ruling the first house, the individual could have a belligerent and bellicose personality. But if Mercury, ruling the mind, is in placid Taurus, and other planets in signs in complete contrast to Mars, judgment based only on appearance may be far from correct. The personal chart provides a complete blueprint or x-ray through which all qualities and conditions of life can be known, so the astrologer should not leap to any conclusion simply on the basis of first house characteristics.

By knowing the nature of Mars, however, it is possible to know those qualities, both constructive and destructive, of one who has the sign Aries on the first house cusp, or, for that matter, on any cusp. Regardless of where this Mars-ruled sign may be placed, all matters in connection with that part of the life will partake of the nature of Mars, fortunately or otherwise, according to the aspects from other planets in the chart.

Because Mars is the natural ruler of the first house sign, it is characteristic of what the first house period of life may be in each individual life. This first period consists of the preschool age, the period from birth to the age of seven, during which the child shows aggressiveness, desires to explore new frontiers of his environment, has much energy, and, if Mars is afflicted, is belligerent, destructive, quarrelsome and hyperactive.

Since Mars is the natural ruler of this first period of seven years, in all children this is the period when the Mars qualities are most evident. In these years, each child seeks to express himself, to dominate others, to move into new situations without feeling the restraint of his elders. Then, as at no other time, he takes on the qualities of Mars in the manner in which he conducts himself, no matter how docile he may become later in life.

It should be noted parenthetically that each house partakes of the characteristics of both its personal ruler and the natural ruler of that part of the chart; both rulers should be considered in any interpretation of the birth chart. The significance of only a single part of a personal chart may be learned, however, by knowing the natures of the individual house-ruler and the natural ruler. It is only through combining all twelve parts of any chart and interpreting them in order of their importance, that the astrologer arrives at a clear picture of the complete personality, the conditions of the present life, and the pattern they will follow.

Second House: Taurus

Before taking up the interpretation of the natural second house, which is under the rulership of the sign Taurus, one fact must be accepted if the interpretation is to be accurate in any way. The sign Taurus, whatever books may say to the contrary, is *not* ruled by the planet Venus, the natural ruler of Libra. It is ruled by the earth, our own solid, fixed planet.

The second house rules the period of life between the seventh and fourteenth year. Could this ever be thought a time reflecting the nature of Venus? In no period of the child's life, from birth to maturity, is he or she so likely to be awkward, unattractive, antisocial, and lacking in the qualities Venus gives. Sometimes these are physically difficult years for the preadolescent, when life is filled with growing pains, lost front teeth, inhibitions, and youthful problems. There is neither beauty nor grace in the child at this age, and little of romance and self-giving—all Venus attributes.

Taurus, on the other hand, is of the earth—earth-bound, intensely fixed in opinions and ideals. The Taurean expresses the desire for material things in the same way the child in this period begins to accumulate possessions: to give him a feeling of importance and security. The second house also expresses this idea. It is the house of possessions and earning ability; the native with many planets herein puts great importance upon what he can earn and add to his store of goods.

No matter what planet may be ruling the cusp of this second house—whether it be Mercury, Jupiter, or

Saturn—it is the revelation of that individual's attitude toward all material things.

Just as Jupiter ruling this cusp may, if badly aspected, bring many possessions which prove to be a burden by their very profusion, Saturn here in the personal chart may give so few desires that there is little in the way of material wealth, yet often great contentment, since he who desires little feels that he has enough under conditions others would consider poverty. The fixed and permanent nature of Saturn, well aspected, also will permit the individual to retain all that he gains and thus live in security, even though the way it is earned may not be easy.

Many rich in possessions are far from content; therefore a fortunate second house in any chart is not always the indication of great happiness. The symbol of Taurus (often interpreted as the head and horns of a bull) is, in fact, the upcurve of the crescent Moon set upon the circle of full form. This is also the position of the uplifted arms begging always for more for the self, symbolized by the circle.

Like the Taurean, the child between seven and fourteen is at that period in development where getting more and more for the self is the greatest urge and the greatest satisfaction. Aries often destroys what has been given, but when the child reaches the Taurean stage of development, he wants not only all of his own toys and material possessions, but often those belonging to others. While Aries is the expression of "This I am," Taurus expresses "This I have."

The seven-to-fourteen-year-old child resembles all

Taureans, too, in the delight he takes in food. This is the age when eating is one of the chief pleasures of life, and the intake of food is plainly one of the important factors in his contentment. Taurus seeks to satisfy the desires of the self. From every standpoint the qualities of Taurus may be seen as those of earth, not Venus, though it seems to be taking astrologers many centuries to accept this important fact.

Because Taurus is fixed, materialistic, and concerned with things rather than knowledge, this is seldom the age when mental activity predominates. It is the period of material self-growth, when the child becomes an adolescent.

Since Taurus is one of the four fixed signs, and represents fixed earth, the child who has, in Aries, expressed the nature of the soul (since Aries is one of the cardinal signs) now needs to express the self in his desire and choice of things. What he will accumulate depends on the sign in which the earth is placed in his personal chart. This placement is always in the degree and sign *exactly opposite the Sun* on the date of birth. Thus, one with the Sun in Taurus would have the ruler of his solar first house in Scorpio, and much emphasis is put on the material possessions gained through marriage (or the lack of them if the earth is afflicted by other planets). One with Taurus on the ascendant and the natal Sun in Pisces would have the earth in Virgo, and so on through each sign. But in every instance material possessions concerned with the house directly opposite to that in which the Sun is placed, will be of great importance to any Taurus individual.

Third House: Gemini

What Gemini rules is more obvious than in any other sign. In adolescent age groups, between fourteen and twenty-one (the Gemini age period), one may see so many of the characteristics of Mercury that there is no difference of opinion in regard to this rulership. The qualities of Mercury are the qualities of restless Gemini. This is the period in which the mind gains most of the knowledge it wishes to use.

The restless nature of Gemini leads the individual with this third house sign on the ascendant, or with the Sun in Gemini, to wish to be always on the move, going somewhere, anywhere, if it means a change of thought, place or circumstance. Notice how the average citizen of the United States, which has Gemini ruling the first house in the national chart, likes travel and change. So, too, do all adolescents interested in cars and means of travel of all kinds, useful knowledge, the goings-on in the immediate neighborhood, and all forms of communication, especially fairly short journeys or contacts with close neighbors.

The Gemini reads, visits, and communicates in all possible ways with those who may supply him, not with a new philosophy of life, but with practical information and knowledge, This knowledge he puts to use either to facilitate his own interest or to exchange for other ideas which may prove useful. He is not concerned with abstract knowledge. He wants to know only those things which may be immediately converted to his own use.

To know what kind of knowledge this type desires, one must look for more details in Mercury's position by sign and house. This will reveal the type of practical knowledge desired and how it will be applied.

If Mercury is in Taurus and rules the third house, the mind is practical along lines which have to do with earning an income and accumulating money—assuming, of course, that Mercury is favorably aspected. If the Gemini-ruler is in its own sign, this individual is always on the go and interested in everything which concerns third house affairs: transportation facilities, what the next-door neighbor is doing, the local papers, letters and telephone calls.

The following three rules get to the core of any situation in which an answer is sought in the astrological chart. First, observe the nature of the planet ruling the sign on the house cusp, for through this can be known the nature of the sign. Then consider the age period which this sign rules. From the example of the interests of those periods from birth to age twenty-one, one may judge the quality of the thought and the kind of activity characteristic of a group, or individual. Finally, consider the dispositor of the planet which rules the house. Mercury in the sign which rules Mars is very different from Mercury in Scorpio. The native with Mercury in Aries is likely to be mentally attacking someone or something, in the aggressive way of Mars. Having Mercury in Scorpio suggests that one is likely mentally to seek to destroy completely some already established and accepted concept, in the hope of replacing it with a new and better one. Having Mercury in Taurus indicates that one thinks in terms of earning and accumulating substantial amounts of money. The native with Mercury in Cancer centers thought in the home, in the maternal attitudes, in the concept of the home as a spiritual point to which the Cancer clings mentally with the tenacity of the crab.

To have Aries on the ascendant makes one personally active or aggressive, but when Mars rules the natural house of Mercury, no matter how peaceful and seemingly disinclined toward aggression the individual may seem, he is always prepared to make a mental, verbal, or printed attack upon whatever opposes his concepts or will.

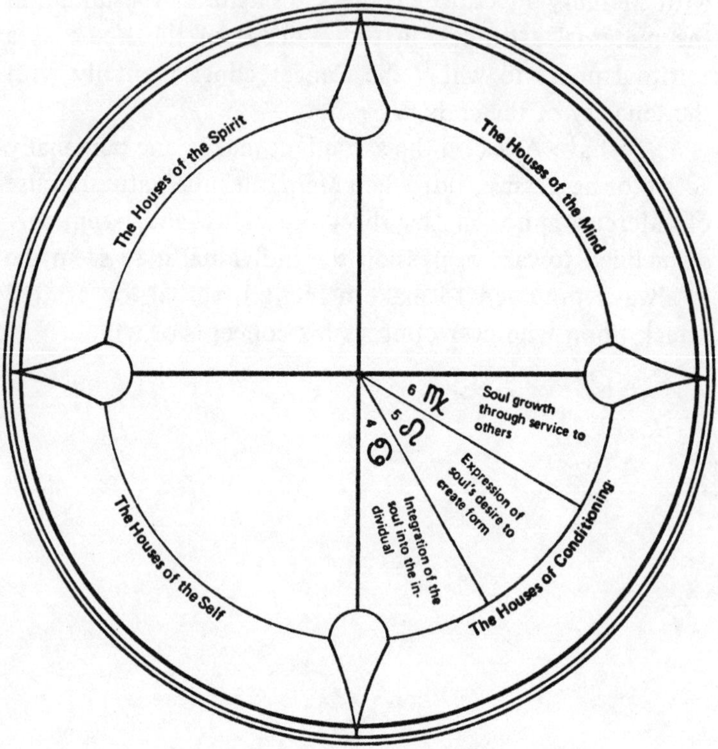

The Houses of Conditioning

9
The Houses of Conditioning

Fourth House: Cancer

The fourth house in the solar chart is ruled by the Moon, as ruler of the sign Cancer. The Moon is ruler of the etheric form of man, not the actual or mortal form, but the emotional, motivating principle. Therefore, this house, usually interpreted only as the "home" in childhood, is, in a sense, the spiritual "home" and its conditions, rather than a location or place of birth or early residence.

The fourth house should be studied to determine what is the nature of the home, not to learn whether it is palatial or poor, but to discover what might be called the spirit of the original home, the first influence felt by the child after birth.

If Jupiter is in the fourth house, or if this expansive and beneficent planet rules this house, the home, no matter how humble it was, offered the child the opportunity for expansion of soul, benefit, benevolent attitudes, and often, of course, also the material benefits associated with Jupiter.

If, on the other hand, Mars is in or rules the fourth

house, it is apparent that discord, conflict, and other Martian qualities prevailed on the impressionable etheric body of the child.

So far as the individual self is concerned, the beginning of the physical life may be read through the planets in the first house, or the sign on the cusp of this house. But the nature of the environment and surroundings, the circumstances into which he is born, is shown by the fourth house—the first house of the second trinity.

This second trinity, sequentially ruled by the signs Cancer, Leo, and Virgo, reveals the qualities of conditioning, not the qualities of the physical self.

Cancer is an ever-changing, restless and emotionally susceptible sign. Its nature is qualified by the position which the Moon holds in the birth chart. First the planetary ruler of the fourth house should be studied, and then the position of the Moon by sign and house. In the natural solar chart the Moon is always the ruler of the fourth house. In a chart where some other sign rules the fourth, the Moon also affects the conditions which prevailed in early childhood and immediately after birth.

Psychiatrists might make good use of this fact, since they acknowledge the part which early environment and childhood impressions play in shaping adult attitudes. With the knowledge that an intelligent interpretation of these three conditioning houses gives, the psychiatrist would discover much that contributes to the maladjustments of personality that become a problem of mature life.

Astrology proves how completely and, in a sense,

unknowingly, the individual takes on the nature of the conditions, harmonious or otherwise, with which he is surrounded and conditioned from the first months in physical life.

Like the ever-changing Moon, which itself is influenced by the continuous change of aspects from other planets, the home is more subject to changes of emotional attitudes than any other part of the infant's life. There are days of discord, of unexpected turmoil in the affairs of those with whom the young child is in close contact, or of greater harmony and opportunity, of happiness and again of disappointment and frustration. These emotional attitudes are reflected in the disposition and conduct of those in his immediate environment. It should not be assumed that because the very young child cannot vocally express his reaction to grown-up attitudes, he is unaware of or untouched by them. Even an animal reacts to changes of emotion in the tone and in the etheric body of persons in contact with it, and is afraid or encouraged by these indications of that person's mental and emotional state.

All experience in physical form begins in the home. From the moment the infant leaves the more stabilized environment of the hospital, the conditions of the home impress themselves on his soul and sensitive etheric form. If in that home there is lack of benevolent attitudes, continued discord, fear, antagonism and conflict, the young child absorbs these emotions and becomes disturbed, neurotic, and emotionally unbalanced. He reflects all qualities which are a part of that first environment.

With the first impression of the soul in its present incarnation, it is conditioned for the full period of life. Such impressions are stamped permanently upon the etheric form, or the inner man through which the physical self functions and draws its subconscious ideas.

Not only is Cancer the sign that marks the birth of soul qualities, it is the sign which, in the personal chart, relates to the mother. This rule may be astrologically verified, in spite of the many controversies regarding it: the parent who is first brought into complete contact with the child belongs astrologically to the fourth house, and is indicated by the ruler and its aspects. If the mother dies or is separated from the child at birth, and the father or some other individual replaces her, then the fourth house will designate the father, or mother-substitute. In all other cases the mother's influence is indicated by the ruler and the aspects to the ruler of the fourth house.

Thus the fourth house is the part of the chart which shows both the nature of the individual who conditions the new-born soul to the circumstances of the present life, and the emotional attitudes which result from the home environment during that period. When the fourth house in any chart is analyzed, the student may know the influence which resulted from the maternal attitude during the period of gestation and at the time of the child's birth.

More than to any other thing, men and women cling to associations of the home. Those associations become either emotionally dear or emotionally distasteful, according to their value in the earliest days. This attitude shows the tenacity of the Cancerian in holding to what it first contacts and his impressionability in reflecting such conditions, either for good or ill. The influence of both the home and the mother are tremendous in conditioning the child, for from them the new life must find its potentials for future growth. Physically, emotionally, and mentally, the child reflects the mother's attitude at the time of its birth. No matter how that attitude may change thereafter, the first impression is forever stamped upon the etheric body and relayed to the physical self. Planned and welcome parenthood, therefore, ought to be the first consideration, if the incoming wave of souls is to know completely constructive conditions for better evolutionary growth.

To see the lasting imprint of the first months and years is to understand more fully the important relationship between the soul or etheric form and the self. The soul communicates to the self its subconscious knowledge and awareness, compelling it to express—as its own personal attitudes—beliefs and qualities of being which the soul conceived in the earliest period of physical functioning.

Fifth House: Leo

The fifth house is the second of the trinity of conditioning, and reveals conditioning in the sense of personal growth through emotional expansion.

In Taurus the growth of the self is seen through material things: food, clothing, all things which serve the physical self, and which the child needs to sustain life no matter where it may live. Life goes on if the material necessities are supplied, regardless of what the environmental conditions may be. Conditions, which are of the second trinity, determine the manner in which the individual grows through emotional experiences. Therefore, the fifth house is the point where the second phase of the development of the soul may be observed. This is a further extension of the emotional environment in which the soul comes to maturity and gains its permanent attitudes.

This stage of soul-growth does not result from conditioning by the mother or the home, but from the expansion of consciousness resulting from all forms of emotion. *The fifth house is therefore the key to all complexes. It shows what controls the emotional nature.* Within the quality and nature of the sign ruling the fifth house can be seen the nature of the reaction the individual shows to every situation in life. This may appear to be a broad statement, but it is accurate.

If the fifth house holds, or is ruled by, planets indicative of abnormal emotional attitudes, it produces maladjusted ideas toward whatever the fifth house rules—sex, children, creative work, education, entertainment, speculation. All take on the quality of the planet ruling this house and/or the planet within it. Because of some emotional experiences in the very first months of life, or even in the previous incarnation, the personality is so stamped with the characteristic attitude of the sign on the fifth cusp that it will be out of line with ordinarily expected emotional attitudes. It has been conditioned in a way which produces discordant or abnormal reaction for the whole of the present incarnation.

Thus the fifth house reveals the underlying principle on which any individual acts in connection with all sexual, emotional and creative thought, since this house has to do with both the creation of form, as in the creation of children, and the production of mental or spiritual creations. All creative activity will stem from the motive indicated by the sign on the fifth house cusp and be done for the purpose indicated by the sign ruling this house and the aspects to its ruler.

Those who look at astrology in a somewhat casual way sometimes call this fifth house the house of love affairs. For some individuals love affairs are romantic, glamorous, happy or beneficial, but to others they bring shame, tragedy, disaster and great unhappiness. The reason for this difference is found in the nature of the ruler of the fifth house and the planets therein, and the aspects to the ruler and planets, as well as the quality of the sign in which such planets are placed.

By studying the fifth house, the student of astrology will learn to appreciate the emotional capacity of the individual and understand its limitations; for the native acts and thinks and feels emotionally only through the nature of the planetary ruler of the fifth house, and the sign in which that ruler is placed.

Since the etheric form conditions his emotions, the individual reflects the nature of any emotion resulting from the experiences of both the present and the previous lifetime. This fact must be obvious, since this nature is well established long before the child is old enough to be aware of either emotional or sexual experience.

Through the fifth house, astrology reveals the barriers, the challenges and the attitudes of the personality resulting from both conscious and subconscious experiences. *The etheric body carries forward from one incarnation to another the memory of such experiences, so it must be apparent that creative thought and emotional experiences and attitudes in the present life are all conditioned by a pattern established in a previous life. This house, therefore, is a key to the past incarnations and past relationships of the individual.* In it may be seen the reason for whatever seems to be abnormal or out of line with the average concept of conduct and emotional attitudes.

With Leo ruling the natural fifth house, the quality of the self-expressing and growth-producing Sun is the natural emotional state. But very few know only the creative and gracious qualities of the solar force in their fifth house relationships. Many find Saturn ruling here, bringing disappointment, bitterness, crucifixion of the soul. Others love recklessly and express the nature of Mars rather than the creative quality of the natural fifth, while the fortunate few with Venus or Jupiter ruling this house are truly blessed through love, children, and creative ideas. Whatever the experience of the past life has been, the subconscious memory conditions the soul to look for and find this same sort of experience in the present life, and unless the individual corrects and reconditions his own attitude, he will continue to find more such experiences in each incarnation.

By recalling through the subconscious faculty of the etheric body what he experienced in another life, he meets present experiences according to what he has learned from the past incarnation. As the burnt child fears the fire, the disillusioned man dreads rebuffs he has known in a past life, yet invites them by his own preconditioned attitude.

The sign on the fifth cusp is also the key to what might be called the creative drive of the individual, the power which impels him to creative expression through ideas or action in any form. He is aware of this power and, knowing himself capable (from the knowledge conveyed through the inner self), he uses it to accomplish whatever objective he desires to attain. This could be romance, creation of form or spiritual and inspired composition resulting from expression of non-material planets.

The period of elementary schooling also is ruled by the fifth house. Each child grows mentally and emotionally according to his own fifth house attitudes, so one should take note of these, in relation to the planets ruling the fifth house. It is seldom through the discipline of Saturn or the expansive quality of Jupiter, or the practical quality of Mercury, that the child comes to know greater truth, but through whatever sort of emotional activity the soul demands in this period of its search for greater self-expression through facts, words, and deeds.

Whether growth is the result of Saturn's discipline, of Jupiter's expansion of the self, of Venus' desire to give selfless service to others, or of Mercury's reading, speaking, and application of practical knowledge, each is educated according to his own emotional attitudes. It is only because children are compelled to attend school for a definite period that many subject themselves to any form of education, and only through their fifth house attitudes will school offer much of value to them.

Educators might do well to discover what the emotional attitude of each child is, since this is expressed throughout the formative, environmental years. Those who may be poor in routine work and unable to respond to classes in subjects which depend principally on memory, may be superior in spontaneous, creative thought which comes from knowledge stored in the subconscious. A child loving approval and popularity will delight in school because of the personal or social contacts it affords. Few attend because they enjoy the routine, discipline, and order characterized by Saturn.

Sixth House: Virgo

The sixth house is the natural house of Virgo, the sign ruled by Vulcan (now called Icarus by astronomers). This latest of the planets to be discovered is the one which, at one period in its orbital revolution, comes closer to the Sun than any other planet, including Mercury. Vulcan was lame and underprivileged, but the only industrious and useful Olympian immortal. He was cast forth from Olympus because, according to legend, as a cripple he was less perfect in form than Jupiter demanded his offspring should be. Vulcan compensated for his own personal lack by giving greater and better service to all gods and mortals than could have been hoped for from one who was, in spite of his handicap, still one of the gods.

Vulcan, like those of the sign Virgo, served in spite of his exalted position, because he delighted in the perfection of the service he gave, not because service was demanded of him. The quality of the workmanship he put into the weapons and ornaments he created for other gods and for a few mortals was so fine that they were desired by all. Vulcan created beauty with perfection of detail, not to please those whom he served, but to put into form a creation which compensated for his own defects. The Virgo individual has this desire for perfection of service in whatever he does, not to win praise but to compensate for what seems, to critical judgment, to be a lack of perfection in himself. Many of those who seem flawed manifest this same pursuit of perfection and do work far more satisfactory than is done by others.

Through the sixth house, the Virgo individual serves the world in accordance with the nature of his own past experience. The subconscious mind remembers the delight, the satisfaction and the spiritual rewards of giving more than others give.

If, however, there is a sign on the cusp of the sixth house which indicates that all service is seen as drudgery, misery, imposition or in conflict with other interests of the life, the etheric soul will express this attitude. That individual proves a poor servant, and since "as one gives, he receives" from others, he will be poorly served. He does work which gives little satisfaction, for his soul, through past experience, has failed to find happiness in serving.

Thus from the three houses of the second group the student may read the nature of the soul's growth. Those who would know the experiences of the past incarnation should study the fourth, fifth and sixth houses in order to discover what created the present mental and emotional attitudes toward the home, toward all fifth house matters, and toward service to others.

These are facts which the psychiatrist must spend many hours of analytical examination to discover. With the natal horoscope revealing these things, the astrologer is in a far better position to appraise the quality of the etheric nature resulting from previous incarnations than any professional who must depend upon personal interrogation to account for maladjustments of the personality. The horoscope reveals, in a few moments' time, what the self reveals over a long period of time through psychoanalysis: proof of the hidden life deep within the subconscious, communicated indirectly through the conscious mind.

The three houses of conditioning account for the attitudes on the part of many who have had no experiences accounting for reactions shown in the present life. The lessons learned by the soul or etheric principle show past development which conditions the personality to proceed to higher evolutionary form upon the basis of experience in past, not present, incarnations.

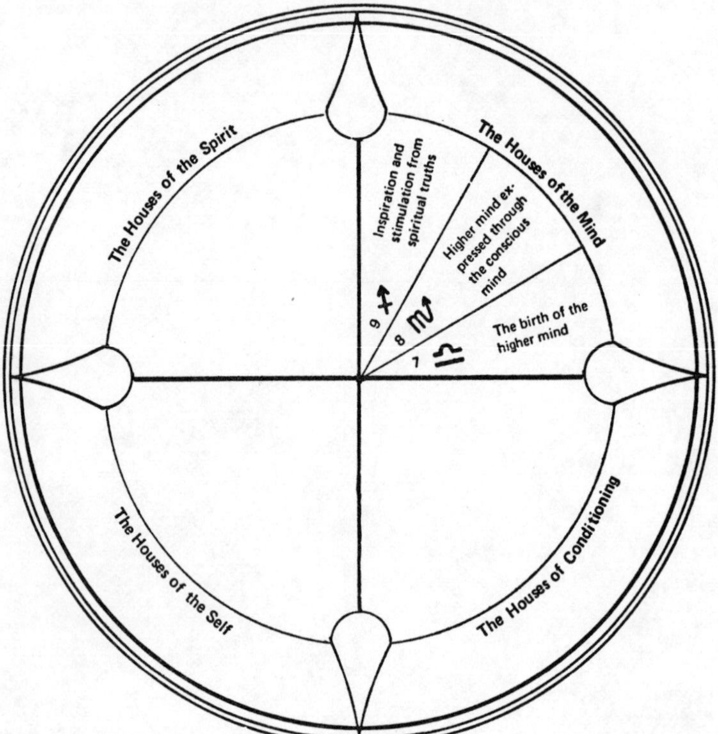

The Houses of the Spirit
The Houses of the Mind
Inspiration and stimulation from spiritual truths
Higher mind expressed through the conscious mind
The birth of the higher mind
9 ♐
8 ♏
7 ♎
The Houses of the Self
The Houses of Conditioning

The Houses of the Mind

10
The Houses of the Mind

By the nature of the six houses between the point of physical birth, Aries, and the point which is the termination of the sixth house, Virgo, man grows toward greater perfection of spirit through those personal relationships which are a part of almost every life. Having grown through those commonplace experiences, he begins what is a graduate course through the six houses above the horizon in the individual chart.

The first trinity develops the self, the physical form and the conscious mind through mental discipline and instruction, plus actual experience. The second trinity gives the soul the chance to grow toward perfection through expressing the emotional attitudes gained through previous life experience.

Seventh House: Libra

At the seventh house, which in the natural solar chart is Libra, the growth of the higher mind starts. At this point man begins to gain knowledge through association with another rather than through his own limited experience.

Because the seventh house is the house of marriage and legal partnerships, it is the first step in a wider education of the soul. By coming into contact with the opinions and viewpoints of another, the soul gains knowledge which would otherwise be outside its scope. Man knows what he has read, seen, heard, done and learned in every way available to him. But much is beyond his range of experience, and therefore can become known to him only through some other individual's knowledge, made available to him through close association. Obviously the experiences of a man differ from those of a woman. Therefore marriage, since it brings a man and woman together in close mental and personal companionship, increases man's knowledge of the way a woman thinks, reasons, acts, and learns through her own experience; it gives a woman who is married greater knowledge of matters which concern a man and are ordinarily not a part of a woman's life.

When each partner has the chance to express his opinion (which is likely to differ from that of the other person), each learns what he would not otherwise know. Therefore a new capacity of the mind comes to birth—the ability to reach beyond the frontiers of the self and learn those things which result from contact with another mind, or with many minds, since the seventh house is also the house of the individual's relation to the public.

Through these interrelationships of mind to mind, each mind should, and sometimes does, reach a balance between thought of self and thought of another. This is the beginning of the development of selfless thought which is, in the first analysis, spiritual thought.

Although Libra offers opportunity for mental growth through contact with another type of mind, it is still mental growth based, for the most part, on a personal relationship. It is not occult nor is it derived from other planes.

Eighth House: Scorpio

Not until the eternal soul incarnates in the occult sign, Scorpio, is contact between the conscious mind and the superconscious mind made. In this eighth house sign man integrates into the conscious mind thought that comes from other planes, or from discarnate minds, whether that thought be constructive or destructive.

When superconscious power is developed through disciplines which stimulate the occult-sensitive areas of the mind and cause one to be receptive to unseen planes, a channel is created which may be conducive to greater growth of the spiritual nature, or exactly the reverse. The establishment of this channel makes the mind vulnerable to *all* types of thoughts. Consequently the individual is tested in his spiritual development, to determine whether his desire is to know constructive thought, stimulating spiritual and ethical growth, or destructive thought, serving only some material purpose.

Strengthening the superconscious faculties of the mind to receive thought from unseen planes is like strengthening the physical body—the added power may be used to lift the burdens of another or to strike a harder blow against him. At each stage of growth the evolving soul must choose whether its growth will be toward the good or toward greedy self-service.

In Scorpio incarnations, the occult thought gained may serve to entertain the public, which pays well for what seems to be unusual power unavailable to the average man. Such thought may involve contact with black masters who offer practical ideas to those who seek knowledge in order to serve themselves and to gain greater rewards from the world. It may destroy the soul of the one who accepts it, or direct him along paths which lead to the destruction of others. It is power manifested through the mind, but its use depends on the Scorpio's ethical and spiritual development. He may become the inspired speaker who teaches truth without reward, or the well-paid performer who teaches nothing but makes profitable use of his power to contact other minds for many purposes.

The eagle flying high above the earth symbolizes the power of the Scorpio mind to soar above the level of other minds. But the eagle preys upon lesser birds, and a mind inspired by destructive thoughts has greater destructive power than ordinary minds.

Scorpio and the eighth house are the points at which the superconscious mind manifests this power to make contact with unknown minds and unseen planes of thought. The Scorpio incarnations are the crossroads where the individual must decide what use will be made of his power. Only if ethical attitudes compel the individual to make selfless use of his knowledge can the mind attain the inspirational qualities of Sagittarius, the culmination of the mental trinity, expressed through the ninth house.

The occult thought that comes to the Scorpio mind is from mental planes, where both good and evil manifest themselves mentally in equal measure. At this point spiritual power is not the control. Discarnate minds on the mental plane, like the conscious mind, are capable of projecting any type of thought to an individual. Only his personal attitude will determine whether he prefers destructive and evil, or constructive and spiritual contact with the unknown. The power of Scorpio lies in disciplines which stimulate the occult transmutation of sexual power into mental power. Desire on the part of the individual for constructive or destructive power is unimportant, as far as the development of this power goes. He is merely building a mental machine to fulfill whatever purposes he chooses. But when it is finished, he must, in time, convert it either to constructive or destructive use, to selfish or selfless purposes.

Ninth House: Sagittarius

When the selfless course is taken, the progress of the soul is toward Sagittarius, at which point the mind, already open, finds itself inspired and stimulated through thought projected from the spiritual or white brotherhood which serves the Christ. Even here, spiritual truth is offered to some only to be converted into cash by those who prefer wealth to greater truth. But when truth so received is freely given to all without reward, those who teach continue to offer such truth in ever greater measure. From this point spiritual inspiration is the reward for good thought and good deeds. Because of this, Sagittarius-inspired thought is of far greater value than knowledge gained from unseen minds which may be either negative or positive.

Sagittarian thought is a bridge between the quality of the conscious mind and the quality of the spirit. It is never negative, but uplifts and awakens. It prepares the mortal mind for attunement to a world in which all thought must be of Sagittarian quality—the plane of Divine Spirit.

In this sequence of the three mental houses, of Libra, Scorpio, and Sagittarius, the higher faculties of the mind are awakened, man becomes aware of his contact with the unseen world and in time attunes himself to the plane of superconscious thought, receiving ideas otherwise beyond his ken. Through Libra, greater knowledge is gained by close association with another; through Scorpio and Sagittarius, the developed mind gains knowledge from mental contact with either discarnate minds or minds telepathically developed in ways typical of these signs. Unfortunately, to the Sagittarian this contact too often is simply regarded as "inspiration." Few indeed consider this contact to be what it is: the reward earned by those willing to teach truth constructively to others in the way it has been taught by many great teachers of past ages and many faiths.

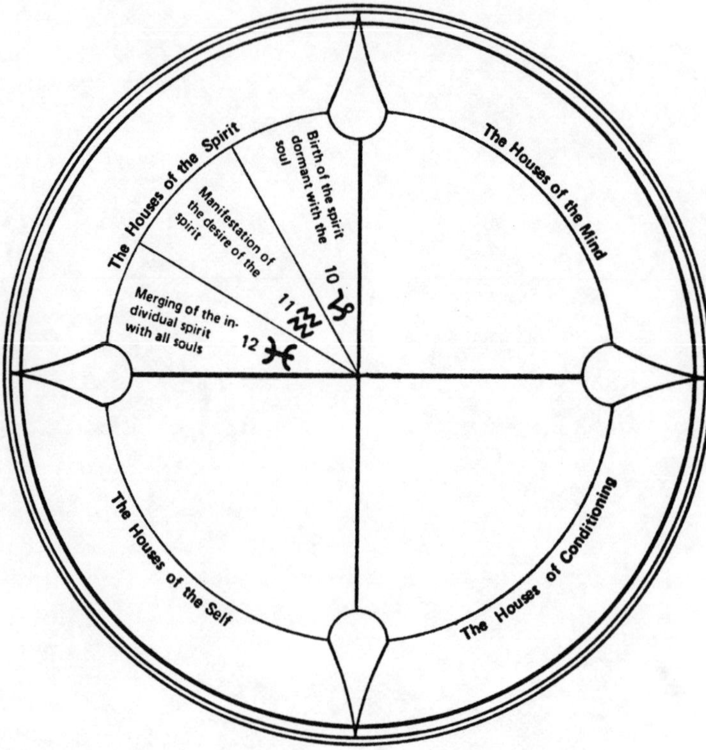
The Houses of the Spirit
Birth of the spirit dormant with the soul
Manifestation of the desire of the spirit
Merging of the individual spirit with all souls
10 ♑
11 ♒
12 ♓
The Houses of the Mind
The Houses of Conditioning
The Houses of the Self

The Houses of the Spirit

11 The Houses of the Spirit

In the final three houses of the chart, man comes in his development to the point where stood the Christ, the Master Jesus, on the mountaintop. Before Him lay the kingdoms of the world, offering all material rewards. But He knew, since He had known inspiration (if He had attained the Sagittarian quality of mind), that there were things of the spirit which might be of far greater value than any reward the world offered. The Capricorn incarnation is the testing point of development where material ambition must be forgotten and the spiritual nature dominate if further progress is to be made. It is the place in evolutionary growth where man accepts the necessity of the unopposed domination of spirit.

In the progress of man's evolution he reaches in Capricorn the contest between the spiritual nature, the indwelling Christ, and what might be seen as Satan, or materialism. Here the Christ is tempted by what Satan represents–Saturn–the principle of form and material substance. Here spirit faces its final temptation by what the world offers through form. Spirit is not truly born until it survives the temptation of Capricorn's ruler, Saturn.

Tenth House: Capricorn

In the tenth house incarnation, spirit and mind conflict. Man has learned through mental attainment in the three preceding signs many things that other men do not know. Now, knowing how well the world rewards such ability, he must be tested once more. With knowledge, inspiration, and the full development gained through the three mental houses, he may gain many things of a material nature. He must make the choice: whether with this knowledge he will seek greater accomplishments of a spiritual nature, or whether he will put knowledge gained through the super-faculties of the mind to material use, thus profiting from "the kingdoms of the world."

Through all time there will be temptation for those who attain psychic, occult, and inspired forms of higher thought, since through such thought a man gains mental power which is of great value wherever it is applied. Man pays little for this knowledge other than in the disciplines imposed upon Scorpio. The Sagittarian gives freely in material ways, for it is in the nature of this sign to assist generously the less fortunate. But as he gives, so he receives. Therefore there has been little material cost to the native undergoing this mental growth. But when the soul comes to the point represented by Capricorn, man often forgets how such knowledge came to him. He prides himself on how much more he knows than other men, and on how much less it cost to gain such knowledge. He realizes that, with it, there are many ways in which he can increase his wealth. So he must decide, at this stage of personal ethical growth, whether to sell to the highest market the knowledge he has come to possess, thereby gaining much of worldly value.

This indeed is the offer of the "kingdoms of the world" in exchange for spiritual truth, since the knowledge did not come through the ordinary channels of education, books, or paid-for instruction. Here is what many will see as the true crucifixion of the soul. The symbol of Capricorn's ruler, Saturn, is the cross surmounting the crescent of etheric or emotional form. On the cross of forced choice between what man wants most and what the soul desires, Capricorn is tortured. The desire of the soul is to continue forward on the spiritual path, while the self thinks only of the rewards of the world. In Libra the higher mind is born. In Capricorn man gives birth to his spiritual nature, when–and only when–the temptation of worldly success no longer crucifies him.

With each of the four trinities there is one sign–the cardinal–in which conditions come to birth. In the first trinity, in Aries, the self is born. In the second trinity, in Cancer, the soul is consciously integrated into the individual. Libra is the birthplace of the higher mind. Capricorn brings to birth the spirit dormant within the soul of each man.

Each trinity shows also the point at which the self, soul, mind and spirit manifest themselves in material ways. In the trinity of the self, Taurus is the point where thought about the self shows in material ways through the accumulation of material substance, the desire for possessions, the demand for money or a source of income. In the second trinity, the soul is expressed in material ways through Leo, and reveals its desire in the creation of children, or of other forms expressive of its longings. In the trinity of the mind, Scorpio is the point where the higher mind is positively expressed through the conscious mind, and occult thought is manifest in words, writing, knowledge or any form of occult power translated into form, words, or action.

Eleventh and Twelfth Houses: Aquarius and Pisces

In the fourth trinity, the fourth fixed sign manifests the desire of the spirit. In Aquarius the spiritual nature of man is manifested through what he does for those less privileged than himself. Here Christ's teaching of "Love thy neighbor as thyself" is expressed in the concept of the brotherhood of man. This is the impersonal thought of spiritual unity with all mankind.

In the final phase of the development of man may be seen the nature of the Piscean spirit. Pisces is the final house of the fourth trinity closest to the nirvana of oriental religions—the merging of the individual spirit in "at-one-ment" with all souls. Here spirit manifests itself through all spirit rather than in individual spiritual attainment. In this sign man returns to the Omnipotent Whole whatever came therefrom when spirit and soul and mind integrated into the physical form and man became individualized and separate from the World Soul. This stage is symbolized in the renunciation of the Holy Ghost—the Divine Spirit in each individual—so that it may merge with the Highest Form and become a part of all souls which are in spiritual form.

The nature of the Piscean soul is completely antithetical to the attitude of Aries, who desires only expression as an individual; thus Pisces is obviously the completion or final phase in the full circle of growth. From the seventh house to the twelfth, this growth has been upward and forward in the circle, as may be seen in the sequence of the houses of the individual chart. In the twelfth house spirit is returned to the Source, to become a part of the Omnipotent Whole.

12
The Use of Transits

In predicting the nature or the timing of an event in an individual or collective life, two methods are used by the professional astrologer. One is the progression of the planets from their natal positions, counting each day following the date of birth in the ephemeris as one year in the life of the individual or the organization whose chart is under consideration. Progressions are very important, for they indicate the periods in the life when those tendencies shown in the natal chart begin to manifest themselves. Transits show much more exact time periods when such tendencies result in action.

For the sake of the beginner, transits might be compared to the working of clock hands over the natal or progressed position of the planets in the birth chart, while progressions could be compared to calendar dates. The latter mark longer periods in the life, but periods during which the clock will point out with much greater exactness the time when the event will occur.

Transits and transiting aspects, even when of the same degree of good or ill fortune, have far less effect if during one transiting aspect there is no corresponding progressed aspect to lay the foundation for an event. During another transit of the same kind, this progressed foundation, having been prepared and being of similar nature, will exert strong influence to assist the transiting aspect.

In one other important way the student must expect effects of dissimilar nature to result from transits forming aspects to the same natal planet. This is the result of the difference in quality of the transiting planet and of the quality of the natal planet aspected. Transiting aspects may act on one of three different levels–spiritual, mental, or physical, according to the nature of the sign in which the natal or progressed planet happens to be. Failure to take into consideration this rather obvious fact results in many shockingly inaccurate predictions in astrology. The amateur, as well as the professional, should always be alerted to the error of predicting changes of circumstances when the expected change may be only a change of mind or of the inner nature.

Since so few authorities have considered this in predicting, it may be well to list specifically the results of differences in quality in either the transiting or the natal planets. In predicting events, the student of astrology should make sure that whatever planet in the natal chart receives some aspect from a transiting planet is likely to bring about events on the physical plane. This natal planet must, therefore, be in one of the four *fixed* signs (Taurus, Leo, Scorpio, Aquarius), since only the fixed signs deal with material conditions.

Just as transits over planets in fixed signs or in aspect

to them cause changes in environment or circumstances, transits in mutable or mental signs bring changes in the mental attitude toward any matter ruled by the planet or the house then transited.

When the transiting planets aspect planets in cardinal signs, some spiritual change or inner awareness results, but it is very seldom obvious to outsiders and not always, at the time, to the individual himself. This, therefore, is the most difficult of all transiting effects to predict if the client expects spectacular and obvious results, fortunate or otherwise. The student should always judge the effect of transiting planets in relation to the quality of the aspected planet in the birth chart, and observe whether the progressions agree in their nature with transiting aspects coming into effect. It is also essential to know the general nature of the results of each type of transit, both by angular relation (aspect) and the general nature of the planet forming the aspect.

Every student of astrology should know the fortunate aspects: the trine (120 degrees from the point in the birth chart under consideration), the sextile (60 degrees) and the semisextile (30 degrees). The trine is an aspect of pure luck, through which, when one understands karma, one realizes that this is the time when the individual has the good fortune to receive back from some source the benefit or profit which he provided for another in some past life, if not in the present one. The sextile aspect provides opportunity to look into the favorable possibilities then at hand. The semisextile logically affords about half this opportunity, and therefore indicates the need for considerably greater effort if progress is to proceed on faster schedule.

The conjunction, formed by any transiting planet within two degrees or less of a planet in the birth chart, is either fortunate or unfortunate depending on the nature of the two planets involved. In a chart in which there is a fortunate natal aspect from Jupiter to some other planet, the conjunction of the transiting Jupiter gives increased benefit, since not one, but two natal planets will feel the expansive effect. If Jupiter in the birth chart has an unfriendly aspect of Saturn, yet receives a conjunction of transiting Jupiter or some fortunate planet like Venus or the Sun, the house which Jupiter rules in the birth chart will be benefited. But when transiting Jupiter is conjunct its natal position, it will be in adverse aspect to Saturn in the natal chart, and there will be overexpansion along lines ruled by this planet. This is because adverse aspects of Jupiter tend to overdo, overextend, or overload one's life in the department ruled by the aspected transiting planet.

Since Jupiter expands and benefits along one of the three levels previously mentioned, Jupiter conjunct any planet brings some degree of expansion to the house this planet rules, whether or not such benefit is offset by unfavorable aspects in the birth chart.

An adverse Saturn aspect, on the other hand, puts added responsibility and a heavier burden on that part of life ruled by the planet it aspects. These are the periods of testing to determine whether the immortal soul has gained sufficient strength to pick up a heavier load and to walk forward without complaints. Yet one must not regard the conjunction of Saturn in the same light with which the square (ninety degrees), the semisquare (forty-five degrees) and the opposition (one-hundred and eighty degrees) is seen. Saturn consolidates and fixes in permanent form whatever it rules in the chart. Therefore, the conjunction is similar to the pouring of the foundations of a new home, upon which the superstructure may be built with every assurance that it will endure. The effect of the square, on the other hand, is to cut out of the life, or prune back, whatever is unnecessary for the fullest development of one special objective or ability, with the result that the usual tendency is to regard an unfriendly (adverse) Saturn aspect as something to dread or fear. Since this aspect delays the development of many plans which might be in mind at such times, it is unwise to expect to complete these immediately if they are started under an adverse aspect of Saturn. Often such projects do not develop at all. Those things which begin or are started under the favorable aspects of Jupiter, on the other hand, can always be counted on to turn out well. It is essential, however, to know the exact aspect under which any project is started if the eventual outcome is to be determined.

In a general way, the square of any planet disrupts some existing condition or puts a hurdle in the way of progress toward the objective; therefore, such periods should not be picked if one wishes to make uninterrupted or easy progress toward a goal. The greatest value of the square is that it brings into the life some new experience which is not in line with the rather fixed development planned by those who think in terms of uninterrupted progress.

Transits of Jupiter deal with periods of growth and

expansion of persons or organizations, while Saturn transits deal with times when development seems to have ceased completely, and responsibilities have increased greatly. The man who works with his personal chart and cooperates with the conditions which come to pass, whether pleasant or not, will wisely start all new ventures under the fortunate aspects of Jupiter to some important and meaningful planet in the birth chart. He will try to avoid undertaking important ventures when an adverse Saturn aspect is coming into operation.

There are also transiting aspects of slow-moving planets which sometimes coincide with fortunate or unfortunate transits to natal planets. These act in somewhat the same manner as progressions, since they are of long duration. The least understood of these is the transit of Pluto, since the outermost planet was only discovered in the 1930s, and not too much astrological research has been done on it.

Pluto is the ruler of the eighth house sign, Scorpio, and the effect of Pluto in transit is much like the meaning of the eighth house in the birth chart. This is the house of death and reincarnation, and transits of Pluto tend to bring to an end some existing condition, mental attitude, or spiritual conviction, permitting it to be regenerated and recreated on a higher level and in better form. Thus a Pluto transit to an important planet in a business chart would suggest a reorganization of the company after termination of present organizational policies. In a personal chart, the present state of things in the life, if the transited planets are in fixed signs, would come to an end and that part of life aspected by Pluto's transit would be cleared of past conditions so that it might develop on a higher level.

Pluto takes almost two-and-one-half centuries to go through all the signs of the zodiac. Thus Pluto's aspects last for some years, and may not form to more than a few of the natal planets in the span of the average life. Due to its position as the ruler of Scorpio, Pluto by transit makes drastic changes in the lives of persons who have many planets in this sign. Such changes are usually disturbing when Pluto transits Leo, in adverse aspect to the Scorpio planets; yet the following transit of Pluto through Virgo, in sextile to planets in Scorpio, brings mental opportunities replacing the conditions and circumstances that died under the unfavorable square from Pluto in Leo.

A transit of Neptune must be interpreted in terms of self-deception, or deception on the part of others. If Neptune unfavorably aspects important planets in the natal chart, it brings illusion, misunderstanding, confusion and misrepresentation. Transits of Neptune in unfortunate aspect form only once or twice in a lifetime, but like those of Pluto, they last for some years and can be disturbing because they are not clearly understood for what they are—conflicts between the material and the nonmaterial planes from which man comes to know both good and evil.

The favorable aspects of Neptune open new paths of spiritual growth, bringing inspiration and psychic thought from unseen planes if the natal planet aspected is Mercury, the Sun, Venus, or the ruler of the ascendant. In such cases Neptune acts on the mind, the spirit, the emotions, or the personality. From the practical standpoint, even the unfavorable aspects are helpful for writing verse, fiction, or inspirational compositions, which may be a source of profit. Neptune deals with illusion, the nonmaterial, the world of spirit, and all that is unrealistic. In all ordinary matters the unfavorable aspect, which forms to some important planet approximately every forty-one years, leads to impractical action due to lack of clear thinking or the inability to distinguish in dealing with others between illusion and reality.

The effect of the transits of Uranus, particularly through fixed signs and aspecting planets in fixed signs, is more dramatic than that of other transits due to Uranus' nature. Uranus, like lightning, strikes without any warning other than that which astrology gives. The result of any Uranus aspect, even the trine or sextile, is always unexpected, unusual, and different from the way in which one has reason to think the matter will develop.

Again and again the astrologer can warn a client to cease to plan, under an adverse aspect of Uranus, for what seems, according to trends, to be a "sure thing." Uranus completely upsets those trends in totally unlooked-for ways which cannot be guarded against. It forces man to try out some new road to gain greatly needed experience—or find himself left without this opportunity for necessary growth. Given free choice, many would only do the very easy and pleasant, or familiar. Therefore, the transits of Uranus come as the lightning bolt comes, destroying a well-established home or business in a moment, compelling the individual so disrupted to start again along some new line of development.

Pluto also destroys the outmoded or valueless, so these two planets may seem somewhat alike in their action. But Pluto is more subtle, and conceals what in time will cause destruction. Uranus acts violently and openly, though unexpectedly. Pluto, being slower in transit, causes many movements and changes which affect large groups. Results due to Uranus are easily observable, because they affect individuals by changing their circumstances; but they also involve literally earth-shaking changes, such as earthquakes that, in a moment, wipe out an entire city.

Like every planet, however, Uranus forms fortunate trines or sextiles to many natal planets during the life. In trine aspect it suddenly opens a new door to an unexpected career or much improved fortune. The sextile brings unlooked-for opportunity for better conditions. Any venture started under a transit of Uranus square to a natal planet concerned with the venture, however, is almost assured of an unexpected termination or unlooked-for development.

Because Neptune, Pluto, Saturn, Uranus, and Jupiter are relatively slow-moving planets, the effects of their aspects are much more marked, since their influence extends over considerably longer periods of time. A Mars transit (though shorter in duration) also produces distinct results, if it is similar in nature to progressions or slow transits in operation at the same time. The transits of Venus, Mercury, Sun, and Moon are likely to mark days instead of longer periods of time, and are of little importance unless they coincide with similar progressions and transits. In such instances, they add emphasis to the indication and come closer in pointing out the exact time when the event can be anticipated.

The effect of the transit of any major (slow-moving) planet is greater when the planet is stationary—that is, when it remains at the same position for a longer period than usual—though the events indicated may happen either before or after the aspect is exact. When a planet is stationary within two degrees of some sensitive point in a chart, it may always be counted on to have some marked influence. It is also important to remember that, should some slow-moving planet retrograde and then return to the same position, its influence is more pronounced the second time the aspect forms.

While astrologers regard all aspects of transiting and progressed planets as an important indication of the time when certain conditions will develop, the most important aspects are conjunctions, squares, oppositions, trines and parallels of declination. One exception to this is the formation of two or more squares or trines by planets in transit at the same time, or close to the same time. In this case the weight of combined influence can produce results from aspects not otherwise considered important.

In general the ephemeral transit of Venus will bring some social contact or add some luxury to the life according to the position of Venus by transit and that of the aspected planet. A transit of Mercury brings letters, increases sales, or marks a period when a journey may be started. The transit of the Sun to any planet increases prestige and honor, if the birth planet is well aspected, or the transit is over Jupiter or the natal Sun. The quickly formed aspects of the Moon mark changes and short trips.

To summarize the rules by which the effects of transits may be foreseen: the student should always keep in mind that transits, even of the major planets, are subsidiary to progressions in operation at the time. Progressions in turn must depend for their effect on indications in the birth chart. Therefore, in considering transiting effects, the student should

- always check the progressions and aspects in the natal chart under consideration;
- notice whether there have been any recent New Moons or eclipses falling on important positions, but allow an orb for the lunation or eclipse of not more than one degree;
- consider first the position and condition of the planet or planets that will feel the effect of any particular transit under consideration, since the way in which the transit will act depends primarily on the condition and place by sign of the natal planets in the chart;
- observe whether the transit is by conjunction, opposition, parallel of declination, square, trine, sextile or some minor aspect;
- look at the planet which is making the transit and check its position in the birth chart and the power it may have for good or evil according to the natal aspects;

- study all transits to see whether they are quick in passing any given point or whether they remain a long time within two degrees, or frequently a single degree, of exact aspect;
- observe the power of a fast transit as reflected in its condition (whether it is free from unfavorable aspects from other transiting planets);
- notice what changes take place in a slow-moving transit from day to day in relation to other faster moving transits to this particular planet, for it is the *weight of agreement* which brings about results. A day when transiting Saturn confirms progressed Saturn in conjunction to some planet in the birth chart will, of course, be less fortunate when stressed by unfriendly aspects of the transiting Sun or Moon, for progressed Saturn has already established a pattern;
- finally, note whether the transiting planet turns retrograde after remaining for several days or weeks in the same degree, since the event is likely to come to a final conclusion at the time the transit resumes forward motion and again forms a close aspect confirmed by the faster moving planets. The previous transit will perhaps mark a step in the direction of the final outcome, but the second, and sometimes even the third time the planetary aspect forms will culminate in the event.

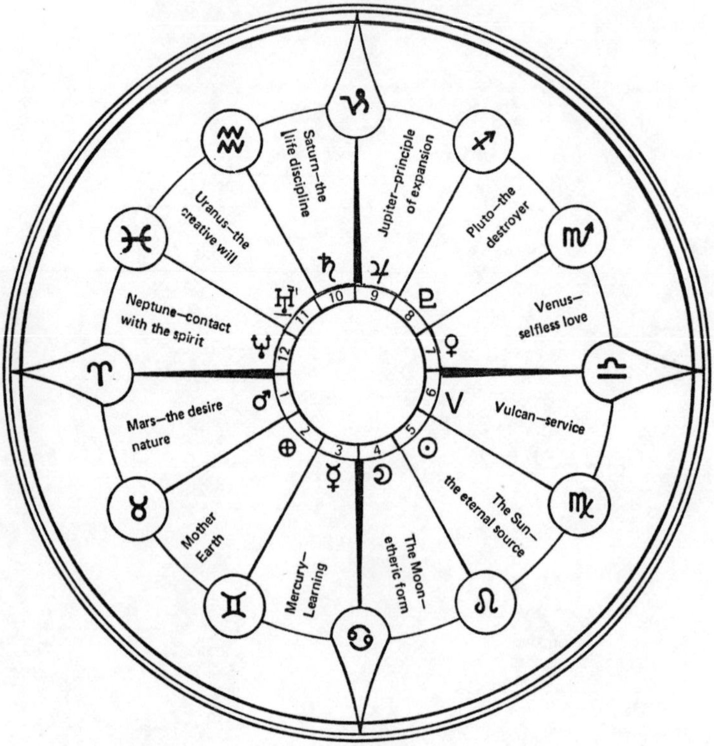

The Wheel of Karma

13
Karmic Law

Those who fail to think that the life in which they find themselves enmeshed is the product of previous existence do not understand the first principle of *karmic law.* While ascending the spiral of evolutionary growth from the lowest form of earth-life to that point at which the monad finds itself no longer needing earth experience, each soul must readjust, compensate, and in every way utilize each earth experience, so that throughout the whole period of evolutionary growth there is equalized, adequate development.

Of what value would it be for a soul to know great agony, great punishment or grievous sorrow, and then pass to another plane and have no further incarnations? Having known only what is designed to test its strength, a soul proves itself strong when it uses such experiences for finer growth, rather than showing frustration over bitter experiences. That same soul, if subjected to triumph, affluence, and temptation in the form of great wealth or wide acclaim must also maintain spiritual balance. Many a man who survives penury with good grace fails spiritually to survive affluence; therefore, the soul is tested through first a life of ease, then a life of poverty. Another testing occurs because many men contrive in all manner of ways to find happiness, yet never succeed, while others born into circumstances that offer little more than the most niggardly return for what is done achieve complete satisfaction.

If the soul persists in denying the purpose for which it returned to life, it loses the opportunity for further development. It necessary, therefore, to transplant it to some other situation, there to test it for further growth. What does not thrive and produce good in the field in which it is planted when first born is either transplanted through force of circumstances or penalized by having to put in preliminary training of an undesirable kind to attain adult maturity once more, in order that it may be tested in yet another way.

Those who study the individual horoscope find ample evidence of each soul's burden in the position of Saturn. If Saturn is in a cardinal sign ruling the second house, the burden is the necessity for that individual to earn an income, even though he may have been born in luxury, since he required such earthly experience. If this is not necessary because of circumstances in the present life, he is truly tempted to evade Saturn's burden, for not only would he be well fed, clothed, and housed without the necessity for work, but he could thus avoid what is, to a certain extent, the spiritual burden the soul carried into the present incarnation.

If Saturn is ruling the second cusp, and in a mutable

sign (Gemini, Virgo, Sagittarius, or Pisces), the individual regards the earning of income as mentally unpleasant, and there is deliberate sidestepping of the idea of being self-supporting, even though the necessity exists. There is a mental block against the thought that money must be earned by one's own efforts.

The third condition occurs with Saturn, the cross to be carried, in a fixed sign. Fixed signs represent the circumstances of life itself. Therefore, if Saturn is ruling the second house and occupying a fixed sign, the burden of self-support must be borne by the individual, otherwise he will starve. He is forced, through circumstances, to follow his spiritual opportunity for growth, and sometimes does this so well that he amasses a great fortune.

In any matter in the life, look for the position of Saturn and realize that this marks the area where the individual must seek further illumination through discipline and restriction. He is exactly like the wayward student sent back for further lessons in a class in which he has failed because he persisted in dodging what was distasteful to his nature, instead of accepting it as a just and necessary part of life.

In order to determine whether a soul has utilized to the fullest extent its opportunities for growth, observe, through the nature of the sign in which Saturn is placed, whether the necessity is mental, spiritual, or physical. In cardinal signs growth is achieved through doing what Saturn demands, not to provide for necessities but to accomplish soul-growth only. This is true discipline, for it is *self*-discipline, not imposed by the circumstances of life.

If Saturn is in a mutable sign, there is a mental disinclination to do what Saturn commands, however necessary that course of action may be. Many with Saturn so placed are individuals who slide by their duty with as little effort as possible and a total lack of enthusiasm for what they are compelled to do.

When Saturn is in a fixed sign, there are circumstances which compel the individual to do what he does or to accept responsibility in whatever part of life Saturn governs. In such situations Saturn permits the inclination of the soul to join with the circumstances, and, in a way, encourages a successful termination of the experience, showing that by accepting Saturn's discipline the individual accomplishes what he desires. What happens, karmically speaking, when one who has Saturn set like a sign along the road of the present life, sidesteps necessary responsibility, discipline, restriction, obligation and duty? Either that soul has to return again to similar circumstances, or steps must be taken within the present life to ensure full settlement of the karmic obligation before progress is possible.

Therefore, when Saturn is seen pointing the way to Calvary, it is not wise to turn from what may seem the place of crucifixion.

14
The Sun
The Eternal Source

If, as some astronomers assert, whenever astrology is mentioned, the belief in the influence of planetary rays is nonscientific, then astrology should be regarded as the art of interpreting truth in a divinely inspired way.

Many men have come to believe that some unseen Power directs all life and guides the course of what man calls destiny. If there is such a Power, is it not permissible for man to investigate this from the proof which comes personally in his own life and in the lives of other men? Following the course of the planets and seeing that under certain conditions in relation to his natal chart, a man makes great progress, while under others he accomplishes less than normal, we decide that by combining experience with knowledge we find patterns suitable for experiment, if nothing more.

Astrology is scientific, however, in that its laws are based on the polarity of positive versus negative attitudes of thought and action. It also accepts the principle that there is a law of cause and effect which works without error from the first and lowest type of form to the final and formless state of mortal life. Astrologers cannot fail, therefore, to believe in the law of karma.

Through karma man becomes aware of cause and the effect resulting from cause. Cause, perhaps, is unseen, but we can in the personal chart observe the effect resulting from cause, and from this infer what the cause may have been.

Problems found in the personal chart are the result of whatever the person did or failed to do in a constructive way in some past life. If in the chart there is great affliction, need we be told that not even the most malevolent Supreme Power would condemn the newborn child if this did not balance his karmic record? There is one version of the Golden Rule which declares, "As you do unto others, so shall you be done by"—not by those to whom one has caused hurt, but by the divine law which metes out impersonal justice.

In most instances this cause came into being in a past life in which the afflicted soul completely exploited the talents given him, and, with a prodigious waste of energy which might have been put to constructive use, spent the precious years of life and accomplished less than nothing. Why else did the Master Jesus tell the multitude how the buried talent entrusted to a servant brought condemnation and punishment from his master?

Nature proves that the powerful law which directs all form demands continuous growth. Therefore, the soul given special gifts which could be constructively used must use them, or in some later incarnation be destined for discipline and retribution.

Heavy afflictions registered in a chart, resulting from a past incarnation of indifferent or destructive living, should not seem unjust. The law of karma is the utmost in justice. Therefore, heavily afflicted charts show astrologers the failures or abuses of opportunity the particular individual is incarnated to correct by living under conditions far less conducive to progress.

Many come to astrologers for truth, but few really desire truth if it is contrary to their personal will. The astrologer needs much courage to tell the client with what seem to him unfortunate conditions, why these conditions have come to pass. It is human nature to prefer to learn only what is fortunate and pleasant concerning oneself.

Yet without truth there is little value to a client in the interpretation of an afflicted chart. When such a seeker for knowledge consults an astrologer, he should be told first of the cause which underlies the present unfortunate circumstances of his life. He must realize that it is because of failure to use constructively opportunities in a past life.

It is only through his present opportunity on the mortal plane that the man who owes considerable good to many can pay his debt to souls which were a part of some former life. The afflicted chart is truly a challenge, therefore. It proves that a soul which has failed in previous lives to make fullest use of opportunities is returned to the classroom of earth experience with the chance to make up for what was previously unlearned. The only cause for lamentation is that the penalties of past failure are circumstances far less pleasant than those of the former life.

The client should be warned in time against another weak or indifferent period of growth, and told that in this incarnation it is doubly important to accomplish whatever was previously neglected, since with each failure the soul incarnates in an even less favorable condition for progress. Those who do not make use of the talents with which they were blessed fall further and further into degradation of the soul. Is it not possible that a man, given this insight, might feel that he has greater reason and incentive to live than if he thought that his life was simply a dull, monotonous routine for which there seemed no adequate reason?

The Sun: Source of Spiritual Growth

Each soul requires different conditions for perfecting growth. The student of astrology must look to the nature of the sign in which the Sun, or monad, is posited to determine how strong such a soul may be in its will to grow, for in each sign there is the potential for growth.

Charts with the Sun in signs from Aries through Libra are those evolving monads learning lessons of personal relationships. In signs from Scorpio through the upper part of the circle of the houses, the soul might be said to be enrolled in collegiate courses of an impersonal nature, to learn philosophical attitudes toward life.

Sun in Aries. The Aries soul, in that Aries rules the first house sign, is like the soul of a child. He does not manifest the thought of the spiritual plane from which he came into being, but feels he is in a world of his very own. So he is brave, bold, intrepid, and lacking knowledge of the conditions he may meet: he is dauntless. He does not know fear because he lacks experience in many incarnations of mortal life.

Sun in Taurus. In time, however, and after many eons of life on the mortal plane, the Aries person learns some caution. He no longer rushes forward in courageous approach to the unknown, but grows conservative and starts to accumulate as much as can be safely gained to assure future security. Thus he goes from the nature of the first sign to that of Taurus, the second.

In the long series of Taurus incarnations, the soul gives much thought to cautious consideration of the unknown, the conservation of food and its own sources of comfort and well-being.

Consider next the *Sun in Gemini.* Gemini is a mercurial sign assigned to rulership of the third house. This house, mundanely, rules all forms of contact with other minds. Mentally the compatability of the Gemini with all other types is very obvious, yet he is impersonal in the same way Mercury is impersonal, for mind is never the master of this type of man. It is rather the medium through which he achieves greatest growth of his soul. To him it is companion as well as servant, and has been so through all Gemini incarnations. Therefore, we find the intelligent, alert, communicative type of mind which originates only practical, useful and necessary thoughts. Gemini is not the student. He is, instead, the interpreter of the thoughts of those less able to communicate. Thus he knows something about practically everything but less about any special thing. His mind simply skims the surface, removing the cream from the thoughts of others, but will not concentrate on any particular subject long enough to delve deeply and completely. He tends to generalize rather than specialize. Gemini's ruler, Mercury, is quicksilver–unstable, changeable, vacillating, scattered, leaping here and there with the agility of monkeys (which Gemini rules), but never settling itself into the dull, routine drudgery needed to delve deeply enough to discover truth.

Gemini, therefore, is fascinating but could not be called a strong sign for the Sun. Strength is the quality of soul which defies all the world to do what it desires, no matter how much opposition it meets.

Sun in Cancer. The Cancerian, since his sign is part of the lower segment, is less mature philosophically than those whose signs are above the line of the horizon, because through his emotional nature he feels rather than reasons. The experience which he gains through the series of incarnations is that which touches the emotions, not the intellect. Because Cancer is the point at which the spiritual monad comes into quickening, or is born into mortal form, the Cancerian's soul is newborn to earth's lessons. The Cancerian therefore reacts in much the same way as the child–responding to experience with feeling rather than deductive reasoning. Maternal love is essentially love without consideration for logic, and the strength of the Cancerian comes from the soul, not the mind.

Sun in Leo. Pre-eminence is supposed to be one of the attributes of those with the Sun in Leo, and pre-eminence is particularly strong in the ego, so the Sun in Leo makes the individual center his whole life within himself. But self alone is not sufficient. Therefore, Leo is self-sufficient, but insufficient for many of the problems of life, for he fails to see life from the standpoint of others. This is apparent when one considers the great number of those in the entertainment world who have the Sun in this sign. Such persons must be self-sufficient; they must center in themselves; they must see themselves as the center of attention, for so long as they do, they succeed. For the average individual in other fields this attitude is anything but satisfactory.

The soul cannot center only in the self or the first segment of the natal chart, for this is only a point of beginning. Unless the soul expands through contacts with every form of life-experience indicated by the other eleven segments of the chart, it remains small indeed. To see the sign in which the soul is posited is to become aware of the limitation put on it from the standpoint of its nature, just as the nature of a seed imposes limitations on the potential of its future growth.

In any large astrological textbook can be found minute details of the attributes of each Sun sign. These signs may also be known by thinking in terms of the nature of each planet and of the sign which each planet rules. When the chart shows the Sun in one of the twelve signs, the potential of that particular Sun will be colored and limited by the nature of the sign and the planet ruling that sign.

Unhappily for students, considerable disagreement

still exists regarding the rulership of Virgo and Taurus, and some astrologers persist even in thinking that Mars carries the double burden of Aries and Scorpio. Those who observe the nature of Taurus may see that it is more closely related to the planet earth than to the rather impractical Venus. For real insight into the nature of Virgo, the student should read the many allegorical references to Vulcan, now known in astronomical circles as Icarus, the little planet close to the Sun, at which the legendary Vulcan had his forge.

Because the Sun is the soul, the spiritual monad, the point of all beginning, it has great importance. From it all succeding periods of growth evolve. The student cannot judge the potential of growth for any chart until he fully understands the limitations and the capabilities revealed by the sign position of the Sun in each chart.

Sun in Virgo. In Virgo, the nature of the true ruler, Vulcan, is clearly expressed. According to the legends, Vulcan was, of all the gods, the only exalted immortal who gave service to his peers and even to mortals. All that Vulcan, as the natural ruler of the sixth house, has jurisdiction over puts greatest importance upon service. The natural sixth house rules not only the armed services (whose soldiers give their lives in dangerous times to serve the nation), but also the laboring classes and those in lowly service. Would this not prove that the soul incarnated in the sign Virgo comes to mortal experience to learn through such service, and grows in stature in relation to the degree of fidelity, loyalty and efficiency such service is given?

Those with the Sun in Virgo prove their strength of soul in a most difficult role: they must be willing to serve well, while remaining free of shame of the fact that they must be less like gods to prove themselves more like honorable mortals.

Sun in Libra. Libra, ruled by Venus, the offspring of the Neptune-ruled world of spirit, is so lacking in the ordinary strength associated with physical life that those who have the Sun in this sign seldom compete on the same level as other signs. Libra excels in those arts in which beauty dominates, and Librans are often created in form to express the beauty of figure and face. The strength of Libra, so seldom realized, will show in his generous creation of beautiful things for the pleasure of others, not of himself. With the ability to give pleasure to many, the Libra native can consider himself strong only when the creations he offers fill the world with beauty or lift other souls to greater awareness of good.

In each sign man continues to grow through learning every lesson which has any connection with that particular field of experience. This means a prolonged period of schooling. He cannot know every experience in any sign in one, or even many, lifetimes, so he must reincarnate time after time in the same sign, until every lesson of the nature of that sign is learned. This is the law of continuous growth upward, which must be accepted by man in the same way it is in the plant and animal world.

Because souls incarnate into conditions and into signs in which, as in school, a program suited to their needs is offered, those with the Sun in the signs of Aries through

Libra are learning the fundamental lessons of form. They are enrolled in classes teaching relationships to others, according to the nature of each of the six houses of the lower half of the chart.

Sun in Scorpio. When the Sun comes at last to the Pluto-ruled house of Scorpio, all personal lessons must have been learned. Here the Scorpio personal nature must die and self-interest be completely eradicated if the soul is to learn through the higher self.

The quality of *strength* is best shown in Scorpio, disliked by almost every other sign because he conflicts with many and cannot see the necessity of adapting himself to others. He has stronger potential for both good and evil than any other sign. He has great intensity of purpose, terrific drive, potentials for destruction that compete with Lucifer himself, and the zeal to do what he desires to the point of self-destruction. Thus, Scorpio could be considered strong but never good, since good means only the desire for upward growth. Scorpio's desire is to accomplish his purpose, whether that purpose is constructive or destructive.

Sun in Sagittarius. Contrast this with Sagittarius, ruled by the expansive and benevolent Jupiter. Sagittarius is strong in his desire to lift the torch of light to illumine the way for others. The Sagittarius has the zeal of the true messenger of highest thought. He seeks to teach truth from inner knowledge of the soul, and to teach what he believes. Therefore, he preaches his belief, in the hope that he may convert others to his awareness of truth. But his faith has a flaw, for it lacks the discipline of Saturn. Sagittarius is likely to believe that in the world there is only good if in past lives he has known only good. Therefore, in the present life he ignores what others see: in mortal life there is death, destruction and drudgery. Sagittarius has faith, and faith such as this lacks the ability to see cloudy skies as other than glowing with the promise of bountiful harvests.

The Sagittarian grows best, then, only in richest soil. Unless he is lucky, he lacks the substance necessary for his growth. If subjected to the limitations put upon Capricorn, he could not attain faith; therefore, he could not find what for him is the very substance to sustain life. The realities of life are necessary for the earth-born soul, however, so the Sagittarian should be told that even in spite of life's unpleasant realities, faith must continue to light the path he takes and be strong enough to survive the disillusionments and the setbacks which he may find in this mortal life. He must know Saturn's disciplines and denials and still keep faith.

Sun in Capricorn. On the other hand, when the Sun is in the strong Saturn-ruled Capricorn, there is need to teach the necessity for faith, for this ambitious, materialistic, and forthright son of Saturn needs Jupiter's optimism. The nature of Capricorn is to be overcautious, overzealous in guarding against opportunities for others which threaten his own.

Though the Sun in Capricorn is strong for many things, it is weak from the standpoint of spiritual qualities. Those who seek to stimulate in Capricorn spiritual thought set for themselves an almost impossible task, unless in the birth chart Venus or some other planet is in Sagittarius to compensate for the Capricorn's materialistic qualities. Otherwise, Capricorn is strong chiefly in the determination to succeed along material lines.

Sun in Aquarius. Since Aquarius is next to the last sign in the upper half of the zodiac circle, the reasonable conduct of those with the Sun in this sign results from many mortal incarnations, during which a great variety of experience has been gained. Life has been known as bitter, as rewarding, as pleasant, or as agonizing in the many fundamental experiences of the soul. When at long last the evolving soul comes to this sign of universal brotherhood, it may look back, through the superconscious awareness which all Aquarians share, and see how greatly such experience added to its present stature, gave it an understanding of all souls in their upward climb, and made it feel at one with all humanity. With this understanding comes a philosophy truly integrating the mortal soul with the Oversoul.

Sun in Pisces. Present-day astrologers consider Aries as the first sign in the zodiac. But, since mortal form integrates spirit and self, or soul and self, the preceding sign, Neptune-ruled Pisces, reveals this close relationship to the world of the spirit. Pisces is the intangible, spiritual, diffused and nonformed. Souls of the Pisces quality are those nebulous efflorescenses that seem almost discarnate, from the standpoint of most of those now incarnated, since they are still, in a sense, separate segments of the great Oversoul. The Pisces soul is, in many ways, still bound and limited—a reflex of the more masterful, more adequate and all-encompassing quality of the World Soul. Pisces, therefore, is conscious unconsciously. He integrates his own thought with the thought of the masses, and since the masses all too frequently manifest inadequacy, the Pisces is more likely to see the difficulty of life than its opportunity. As someone once truly described this kind of person, "He is happily miserable."

Astrologers often feel that most of those who consult them are still in the segment of personal relationships, however, since almost every client wants to know about one of two things–money (the Taurus second house), or love (the Leo fifth).

This is understandable, since few in the lower stages of evolution are concerned with other than their own lessons. But many things are more important than personal problems, and while astrology gives the real answer to those questions, it ought to be considered as more than a popular form of fortune-telling: it is the key to self-understanding, to unlocking the reason for one's present incarnation in mortal life.

15
The Moon
Etheric Form

Through astrology truth is revealed to man as it is in few other ways. In the beginning there is the spiritual form, the monad, the beginning of all life, the divine spark. This form of beginning is represented by the Sun in a birth chart.

What began as the monad descends through all planes of being, until it reaches that state of involutionary development at which it functions in etheric or lunar form.

The Moon is, in the cosmic sense, the reflector of physical life. Physical life is developed from spirit, through nonform, into form. Gas, for example, is nonform in the sense that man sees form as a material substance of a more or less solid nature. Liquid is form, but nonform to those who think in terms of solid and fixed matter.

The form with which the Moon is concerned is that intermediary (liquid) between vapor and man's present body, which he considers solid. The Moon rules all liquids, no matter how much or how little may be a part of solid matter. Because it rules all liquid, the Moon is the medium through which spirit integrates into matter.

Students of science are aware that gaseous vapors may be absorbed into liquid. This liquid, in which the content of the gaseous vapor was absorbed, may, in turn, be absorbed into any form of dry matter, thus integrating what was originally gaseous form, through liquid, into dry or solid form.

To gain mortal life from what was vapor or spirit, man must go through the process of first integrating the spirit into the lunar, etheric, or liquid form, and then integrating that etheric form into the form in which man comes into mortal birth.

All that comes into being grows toward destruction since what comes into life of any kind is in the process of growth. Growth continues until it reaches the ultimate potential. From that ultimate it must decrease, dissipate and die, to become, in the interval before it begins a new process of growth, formless, nonform, or the constituent of future form. Therefore, the Moon is always the connecting link between the spiritual monad and the physical form.

It works through the liquids in all forms of life, whether those liquids are in the flower, the leaf, or the tree. It is the sap of the tree, the moisture drawn up in the stem of the flower. It is the liquids in the human or animal body.

Before man attains mortal state he is suspended in the embryonic liquid which surrounds the foetus. With vestigial gills, he is almost fish-like in the earliest stage of development. The infant grows, the little unborn animal grows, and plant life grows in a small foetal bed of pure liquid. Without liquid there is no life. As the embryo develops further, liquid is assimilated through the placenta as part of growth. From the very first moment of mortal life, therefore, Moon-ruled liquid surrounds and is within the physical body.

The Moon represents etheric, often misnamed astral, form. "Etheric" is the name by which it should be called, because it integrates the ethers or vapors of the cosmos. All that comes from the many planetary bodies is absorbed into form, figuratively, through the functioning of the Moon. Through its metallic quality and condensation properties these ethers become, in a sense, a part of mortal form. Through this same condensation process, all liquid becomes a part of all form on earth and is integrated into otherwise solid, dry matter.

As an example of the way in which metallic substances condense vapor and change it into water, observe the needle-like metal-covered spires of the great New York City skyscrapers which are high enough to penetrate low-lying clouds. At the base of the building, even when there is no rain, there is often condensed vapor, sometimes so much that it might be mistaken for water poured over the pavement. It comes from condensation of moisture on the metal spire, when that spire is in contact with low-lying clouds.

Think of the Moon functioning in the same way as the metal-covered point—not as fertile earth with porous soil absorbing all moisture from vapor, but as solid matter through which liquid-containing vapor is condensed into liquid and integrated into animal, plant and human life.

Etheric matter might be called the "auric egg." Those who are aware that there exists in all life an aura, know that within mortal form there is another kind of body which is susceptible to many types of emotional stimuli. This auric egg, or aura, is visible to the sensitive in various colors, depending upon the quality of emotion felt by the individual observed at that particular moment. This aura is the lunar quality in the only visible form in which it may be perceived, other than as liquid.

The changing colors of the aura are the reaction of the water content of the human body to the emotional state of the individual at that period.

Just as the human body incorporates certain types of energy which may be measured with instruments, it also incorporates qualities of emotion. Emotion is, in itself, mainly the result of the lunar emanations which change frequently as the other planets form aspects to the earth's satellite. Through these lunar emanations man comes to awareness of the cosmic radiations and their varying effects upon him. He responds to planetary vibrations because he incorporates, through liquid in his own being, the vibratory force of all planets via the Moon. Were there no Moon, man could not feel these vibrations, for solid form is dead, inert, and insensate clay, lacking in liquid to absorb vibratory power.

Those who work with plant life know that through the period of the waxing Moon there is a marked increase in the proportionate rate of growth in all forms of vegetation. This is the effect of lunar force upon one form of life. Through lunar force the plant receives the vibratory power of the Sun. It is known, from long observation, that the Sun produces marked growth in plant life in well-watered and sunny locations. But if a plant is exposed to strong, hot sunlight, and given no water, it will survive only until the liquid that was in the soil and the plant itself is consumed. Then it will shrivel and die.

Without the liquid that the Moon contributes, the Sun would become the destroyer of life rather than the promoter of greater growth. It produces growth only until the liquid content of the plant or animal body is absorbed. Thereafter the Sun reduces to dust the inert form left when liquid disappears.

The Sun supplies power which animates life only when the form is conditioned to handle the source of power. The actual process through which such power is handled comes from the Moon. While the Sun supplies power to all planets of nonform, when any matter solidifies, the solar force and the lunar force must work together.

The Moon in the personal chart indicates the etheric power generated within the individual by the combined qualities of the Sun, the nature of other planetary forms, and the lunar power in which the qualities of other planets are incorporated.

Since the Moon rules both the physical body (through the rulership of the etheric body) and the mother in a birth chart, there is a close relation between any physical form and the mother who gives it mortal birth. Actually the Moon is the mother, for only through the Moon's function and the etheric form may man come to mortal birth.

There is, however, a destructive force in the Moon. It

rules the emotional nature and if the emotions dominate they overshadow the mind. Contrary to popular opinion, the Moon in one of the three emotional water signs is not the mark of a superior psychic—even though it shows a high degree of sensitivity. Unless other planets are in positions which give mental balance to this emotional channel, such a psychic is subjected to every form of emotion from unseen forces. He is controlled by these forces instead of making intelligent use of what comes through the conditioned channel of his nature.

Because of the close connection between lunar aspects and the emotions, the Moon controls man's emotional response en masse as well as individually. Mob response to any situation is the result of lunar influence. Through the continuous intake of liquid, partaken of regardless of planetary lunar relationships, great numbers of persons temporarily incorporate into their own nature the same type of planetary vibrations. If these are destructive, the masss thought and emotion is destructive for that whole period.

It is fortunate that this planetary pattern changes from hour to hour, as aspects from the Moon to planets of different natures change. Therefore, though it can and does influence mass emotion in those periods when it is most dominant, the pattern of influence is a changing one. While adverse patterns endure, however, enough men feel the same emotions to produce mass-action expressing fear, anger, restlessness, and all manner of emotional moods. This is especially true when there are many planets in fixed signs, incorporating, by way of the Moon, the planetary influence associated with the symbolism of Uranus, Neptune, Pluto, Mars, and Jupiter.

Such conflicting ideas and emotions are bound to cause violent differences of opinion on the part of those who are emotionally controlled, and to create periods of disruptive and discordant reaction. It is intelligent, therefore, to watch the phases of the Moon in relation to other planets, and test their correspondence with behavior by taking into the system large quantities of water in the periods of harmony with other planets.

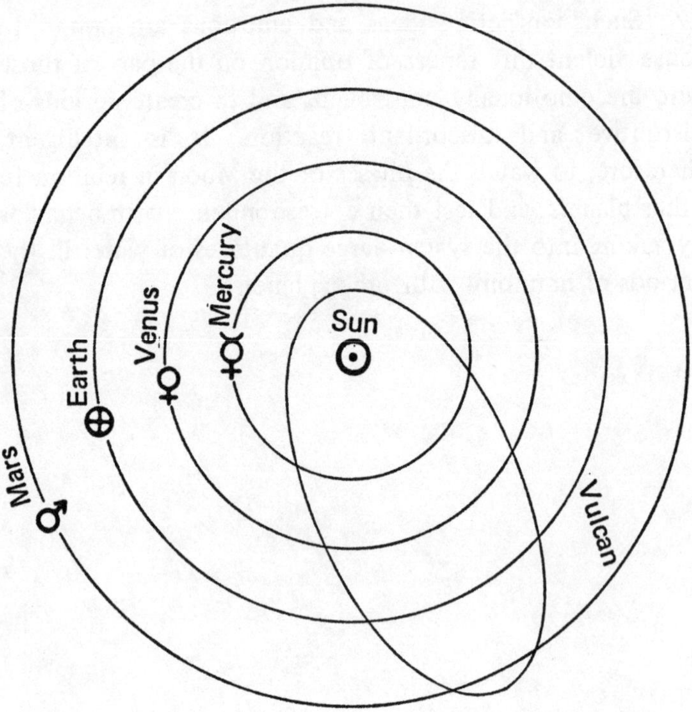

Orbit of Vulcan

Orbit of new asteroid as related to the paths of the four inner planets. Time to complete orbit: 411.8 days.

16

Vulcan and Earth as Rulers

It is almost forty years since the discovery of Pluto, yet some astrologers still refuse to accept this little-understood and distant planet as the ruler of the eighth house sign Scorpio, despite the similarities between Pluto and this house of termination.

This same reluctance to test and accept rulers not known to the earliest practitioners of astrology may also cause some to ignore both the earth and Vulcan[1] as sign-rulers, though both of these planets are far more suited to govern the earth sign Taurus and the earth sign Virgo than are ethereal Venus and restless Mercury.

Like other signs which for a time were forced to share rulership because no planet had been discovered to rule these signs, Taurus had to share Venus' rulership with Libra regardless of a great difference between the earth sign and the air sign which Venus really rules. In spite of our familiarity with the nature of Taurus and with that of our own earth, we seem to have failed to realize their correspondence and logical relationship.

[1] The information in this chapter concerning Vulcan (Icarus) has been adapted from an article in *Sky and Telescope* (Cambridge: Sky Publishing Corp.), September 1949, page 291.

Vulcan Rules Virgo

In recent years one or two modern astrologers have suggested that the rulership of Vulcan over Virgo is possible, but the only book in which this was mentioned was written many years ago by an English astrologer, Isabelle M. Pagan. In her book *From Pioneer to Poet* (London: Theosophical Publishing House, 1954) she speaks of both the earth and Vulcan as possible rulers (page 73):

> The ruler of Virgo is described in astrological tradition as the negative side of Mercury, an expression which tells us that this aspect of deity cannot be positively connected with any known planet. Some recent astrologers have put forward the theory that the true ruler is Vulcan, a planet whose existence is suspected by astronomers and whose invisibility is accounted for by the smallness of its size and its nearness to the Sun, whose radiance eclipses it.

In justification of her theory, the writer refers to classical mythology, the real key to astrological source, which tells of the role Vulcan played among the Olympian gods. He was, it is written, the only one of the immortals who gave any service, and it should be impossible for any student familiar with the nature of Virgo to read what Bullfinch in *Age of Fable* (New York: Tudor, 1936) says of Vulcan, and what this older authority points out, and not feel that most astrologers have been in error for many years in not accepting Vulcan's rulership of the natural sixth house sign.

While I had arrived at this conclusion many years before I discovered a reprint of the then out-of-print earlier edition of *From Pioneer to Poet*, one point is especially significant: the Vulcanalia, the chief festival honoring Vulcan in Rome, was always held on August 23, the day the Sun enters Virgo. Other reasons for feeling that old ideas of Virgo's ruler were in error are founded on the many similarities between what allegory tells of Vulcan and what has always been accepted as the nature of Virgo and of the sixth house.

If we accept what *Age of Fable* calls Olympus, abode of the gods, as our own celestial universe, additional light is thrown on Vulcan's nature and origin in the story of the god's expulsion from Olympus as a result of disagreements between Jupiter, of whom he was said to be a son, and Earth, with whom Vulcan sided.

But before this correspondence is examined, we should also consider what seems to have been completely ignored by all astrologers—the relationship of Vulcan and of the sixth house to weather. Authorities in the past have assigned weather to the fourth house, which of course rules the land. To the sixth house they have given, among other things, rulership of feeding and housing the public. Logically weather conditions do little to change the land itself, but weather certainly does determine how well or ill the peoples of the world will be fed and what type of housing they must have to protect them from the elements. With this in mind, read Hesiod's *Theogony*, which states that Vulcan had three helpers, one-eyed giants called Cyclops. Their names were certainly meaningful. One was named Brontes, which translated means "thunder"; another, Steropes, which means "lightning"; and the third, Arges, "whirling." These are the three elements of weather change that affect human welfare: habitations are destroyed if struck by whirling tornado, crops depend on the rain attending lightning and thunder. These Cyclops were sons of Uranus (cosmic energy) and Terra (the earth) and their special business was to forge thunderbolts for Jupiter, who in his paternal role seems to have had considerable jurisdiction over Vulcan.

One other relationship between the Vulcan of allegory and what the sixth house rules—the armed forces of any nation—may be found in the story of Vulcan's terrible son, Periphetes, a ferocious savage who walked around his father's domain armed with an iron club and prepared to attack all trespassers. What better symbol of the part the armed services play in national defense?

Although Vulcan was born in Olympus, his difficulties with Jupiter caused him to be tossed out of that privileged place in early youth, so forcibly that he fell all the way to earth and landed on the Greek island of Lemnos. Here the industrious but lame god, crippled by the fall, set up his forge and began a career of metal craftsmanship. The sixth house rules labor groups and those who do lowly service for the world. But Vulcan was artist as well as artisan, for in another legend it is told how he "built the palace of the Sun," a magnificent edifice with twelve doors, alternately silver and gold. To do this he also established a forge at the Sun, to which he returned at regular intervals.

Remembering these revealing stories, observe how exactly they fit into the discovery of Vulcan in 1859 and its rediscovery and renaming in 1949. Perhaps astrologers have been indifferent to giving this little planet a place in our universe and a sign over which to rule because of the curious conditions under which it was first observed, its disappearance and the refusal of modern astronomers to think that any planetary body could be found closer to the Sun than Mercury, as Vulcan is at one point in its orbit.

On December 22, 1859, M. Lescarbault, described by his friends as "a simple, small, modest and timid village doctor" who liked to study the celestial bodies with a small telescope, wrote the famous French astronomer Leverrier that on March 26, 1859, he had observed a little black spot crossing the rim of the Sun. By timing it, he found it was visible for one hour, seventeen minutes and nine seconds, but since he lacked the mathematical knowledge to figure the time it might take to complete its orbit, he referred the matter to professional knowledge. Leverrier, according to the long account of this original discovery given in *Myths and Marvels of Astronomy* by Richard A. Proctor (London and New York: Longman, Green, and Co., 1893), went personally to the home of Lescarbault, in the village of Orgeres, to check on the reliability of the discovery and the discoverer. He was so well satisfied that he requested, through the minister of public instruction in France, that Emperor Napoleon bestow upon the little doctor the decoration of the Legion of Honor. In the interval

Leverrier had calculated, on the basis of the time the black spot took to cross the Sun's rim, that Vulcan should return and complete its orbit close to the flaming center of the solar system in about nineteen days. Unfortunately for both Lescarbault and his sponsor, Leverrier, no planet of any size was seen on the Sun's face at the time Vulcan was scheduled for reappearance.

Many attacks were made upon the village doctor and Leverrier by astronomers, though Proctor gives other accounts of such a black spot having been sighted at different intervals by other viewers. But the failure of the small planet to return when scheduled was too much for astronomers to tolerate, and as late as 1948 I was personally told by Dr. Harlowe Shapley of Harvard that there was "no celestial body closer to the Sun than Mercury."

Imagine the surprise of astronomers, therefore, when on June 26, 1949, Dr. Walter Baade, using the new forty-eight inch telescope on Palomar Mountain, found and photographed the trail of a new celestial body, so small that in spite of its fixed orbit, astronomers called it a planetoid or sometimes an asteroid. Instead of giving it the original name of Vulcan, they called it Icarus for the mortal youth who sought, with feathered wings, to fly very close to the Sun, only to die in the fall back to earth when the Sun melted the wax holding the feathers.

But while assigning the new discovery another name, they confirmed, unknowingly, the truth of the original discovery, for it was shown that the orbit of Vulcan/Icarus was not like that of other planets, but much longer—an elliptic which takes 411.8 days to complete, and extends from the very edge of the Sun to beyond the orbit of Mars, cutting the orbit of all the lesser planets and of earth. The original discovery seemed an error, since the time for return was based on the rate of movement of a regular orbit as near the Sun as the place where the small dark body was first sighted.

According to a story which was made available soon after the Baade discovery, the orbit of Icarus is 21 million miles from the Sun at perhelion and 177 million miles at aphelion. Its closest approach to the orbit of the earth comes near its descending node, at a distance of about 4.6 million miles. It reaches this minimum distance from earth every nineteen years, a figure which corresponds interestingly with the Smithsonian Institute's record of weather cycles (on June 14, 1968, when the conjunction last took place, some parts of the nation certainly had remarkably different and unseasonal weather). It might be suggested, therefore, that when astronomers supply the weather bureau (and astrologers) with the exact positions of Icarus (Vulcan) in relation to all other planets or with the time when it passes through each orbit, we may get much more reliable long-range weather predictions and know more about all matters ruled by the sixth house.

Since service was the chief function of Vulcan, persons born with Sun in Virgo, Virgo ascending, or many planets in this sign, seem to be the skillful, practical and efficient employees and craftsmen, delighting in giving high-quality service in any field in which they are employed. Unlike restless and volatile Gemini individuals, truly ruled by Mercury, they are orderly, dependable, willing to follow directions, obedient to superiors. They carry out orders in the same way members of the military forces do, without argument and with great attention to detail. Like Vulcan, who worked alone at his forge, they prefer to do work personally rather than delegate it to others, considering those with less skill incapable of carrying out their ideas. Also like Vulcan, they seem to think less of the reward for their work than the perfection with which it is done.

It is strange that in the allegory of Vulcan's expulsion from Olympus to such a distance, no astrologer or astronomer realized that this might be a suggestion of an orbit which extended much further from the solar center than that of other inner planets. But so few turn to allegory for truth that many half-hidden facts of science, as well as of astrology, might be revealed were legends better understood.

Earth Rules Taurus

The difficulty the astrologer finds in making use of Vulcan for insight into planets in Virgo now is that we have no astronomical ephemeris of this planet's day-by-day positions. This is not true of the earth as ruler of Taurus. The earth is always in the sign exactly opposite the Sun in any chart and at the same degree. Students may check any house with Taurus on the cusp (and therefore Earth-ruled) by the rules which apply to the natural second house, for in matters of the Taurus-ruled house the person or organization will be down to earth, practical, materialistic, concerned with problems like income and earning ability—all these matters connected in some way with the house in which the earth falls in the chart.

The Taurean is indeed a child of the earth, loving nature, and blessed with a green thumb. Taurus often produces beautiful women and handsome men, but the beauty is more earthy, natural and serene than the somewhat artificial loveliness of Libra, though this may be one reason Taurus was supposed to be Venus-ruled.

We agree with Isabelle M. Pagan in her chapter on Taurus when she writes (*From Pioneer to Poet,* p. 22):

> The true ruler of Taurus is probably the angel or planetary spirit of our own kindly Mother Earth, a deity worshipped under many names. . . . In Christendom she has been replaced by the Madonna in her aspect as earth mother, the aspect under which she is pictorially represented as sheltering her children under a long, flowing cloak. The month of Mary is May, when the Sun is in Taurus.

Even more importantly, she is described as:

> the woman of the Book of Revelation, who is said to be supported and helped by the earth which gives her an abiding place in the day of her need and which devours or absorbs those waters—astral energies—which would otherwise have swept her away. She is described as being clothed with the Sun and crowned with the twelve stars and having the Moon—the

> satellite of the earth—under her feet; and she is destined to bring forth at the appointed time the Redeemer of all mankind. The whole of this description is full of meaning to the student of astrology.

So, too, are many allegories, some of the old fairy tales, and most of the parables offered by the Divine Master to those who could only understand simple principles. Until astrologers see in so many teachings of esoteric nature the same facts which they seek to put in scientific form, much truth will be left untouched.

The student of astrology who desires to put astrological rules to the test should insert in all charts the sign for earth directly opposite that of the Sun, therefore, and also note, as he does so, that through whatever house Virgo rules, the person will give service of some kind for the delight of serving, as Vulcan did.

17
Mercury and the National Horoscope

When comparing the quality of Venus with that of Mercury, the student of astrology is dealing with great difference of expression. Mercury lacks the emotional quality of thought. Venus often expresses this in the desire to give spiritual love through some form of art, music, poetry or selfless devotion. Mercury is not, of itself, even slightly spiritual. It is, in fact, more practical than any other planet in the entire chart. While Saturn represents discipline, Mercury is knowledge gained through reading, listening, observing, or doing. It is the quality of mind resulting from conditioning from without, not from within.

Mercury rules whatever man learns for his own benefit, whether it is the child's first lesson in taking a few faltering steps toward what he wants to reach, or the young man's technical course, taken to earn a better income in some field demanding specialized education.

Mercury might be compared to the mercury or quicksilver in the tube of a thermometer—speedily responsive to the conditions by which it is surrounded.

It remains dormant if there is, within its environment, lack of any stimulating thought or experience through which it may grow or expand. But like the mercury under warm temperature, the Mercury-ruled mind, under good aspects of Jupiter or the Sun, grows and expands. Saturn disciplines it and delays its growth. The coldness of Saturn restricts the mind by denying it the opportunity to learn through many types of experience.

Mercury, when in conjunction with, or adversely aspected by Saturn, may indicate less alertness and swift-winged flight than is commonly associated with this planet. The conjunction is always the indication of the disciplined mind, well set in the routine procedures to which it is accustomed. Only when stimulated by planets of the nature of Venus, the Sun, or Jupiter in conjunction or favorable aspect can Mercury in the personal chart indicate great mastery and awareness of a subject.

Mercury suggests, therefore, a personality far better able to grow in practical knowledge if less discipline and more opportunity for experience or expansion is offered. The disciplined mind is better fitted to follow orders and function with regularity, however, once certain procedures are fixed in the mental pattern. For best growth, Mercury needs to be exposed to constructive thought and experience.

In mythology Mercury was called upon for many services in communication between the gods and mortals. He was the messenger of the gods, yet the planet Mercury is associated with all qualities of mortal life. Mercury serves one type of planet and therefore one sort of man as well as it serves any other. It is neither fortunate nor unfortunate except as it is aspected by other planets, since each is served according to its own nature.

Mercury is negative in the personal chart when in negative aspect to a more important planet which influences its nature. This results in a negative thinker, so lacking in constructive ideas that he cannot make a decision without the influence or opinion of another. He is incapable of forming an opinion simply on the basis of the knowledge he has gained through his own limited information and experience.

A Mercury-type person does not really decide for himself. He simply accepts the decision resulting from the influences on him. Therefore the true Gemini, strongly under the influence of Mercury, is more dependent upon all influences on his mental nature than any other type of individual. What his mind becomes is the direct result of what influences his thought, especially if such thought is the result of experience.

The Mercury individual learns through doing. He grows either for good or evil, by doing things which are good or evil. This is because Mercury does not indicate the discipline of Saturn, the self-giving quality of Venus, or the expansive nature of Jupiter. It does not reflect the energy or the desire of Mars. It is simply, so to speak, the messenger between all the qualities of each man and his conscious mind.

The Mercury individual does exactly as he is directed to do. He carries messages from the mortal mind to the self in which that mind functions. Like the messenger who serves Western Union, he is not concerned with the nature of the message he carries, whether it is of good fortune or disaster. Mercury's function is to convey many kinds of thought to the self. The qualities of Saturn, of Jupiter, of Venus, of Neptune, and even the changeable and unusual thought of Uranus are expressed through Mercury. Its function is to deliver whatever type of thought is inspired by other planets.

The quality of all planets in Gemini depends upon its ruler, but the quality of Mercury in each chart depends upon the favorable or unfavorable aspects of other planets to it. Therefore, the nature of the Gemini person will be that of whatever planet aspects Mercury to the greatest degree.

It is not possible, for this reason, to generalize about the quality of Mercury or Gemini, since Mercury is dependent on the aspects from other planets to determine its own quality.

When the quality of the signs is considered, less may be known of Mercury than of any other planet unless the complete chart is considered. When an individual has the Sun in Sagittarius, he is of the nature of Jupiter, no matter how many aspects Jupiter may have in his birth chart. He is like his ruling planet, constructive and expansive–or overexpansive–in a material way. But if the Sun is in Gemini, we know only that Mercury is the ruler of the Sun sign. Not until the student observes what aspects Mercury has to every other planet, and in what sign Mercury is placed at birth, can he judge whether this is the intellectual and brilliant type of Gemini, or the man who uses the qualities of Mercury for the most profitable opportunities without considering the ethical principles involved.

Consider the national chart, for instance, in which Mercury rules the Gemini ascendant. Mercury portrays the type of man who may be considered typical, in his interests and personality, of the American citizen, and also the mercurial nature of the population. Mercury rules the ascendant in the United States chart, and Mercury in the national chart is in Cancer. Thus the nature of the ever-changing and restless Moon is a part of the nature of the common people of the nation—as distinguished from the special groups indicated by two other planets in the first house of the national chart. Therefore, Americans are a restless, unsettled nation, spending large sums on all forms of travel and communication. They often consider a costly automobile more necessary than a home or a college education. They come and go aimlessly because of their mercurial love of change and new experience gained through contacts with neighboring communities, states and nations.

The fact that Mercury itself is in the second house of the national chart (the house of income and material possessions) makes the United States more mentally interested in making money and accumulating possessions than in any other form of activity. (The sextile aspect of Mercury to Neptune in the fourth house suggests a tendency to do everything in this area on a vast scale, for instance, on the level of mass groups.) When many Americans buy a home, for instance, it is with the idea that if they grow tired of it, or the location of their work changes, or the neighborhood is not what they desire, it will be sold for more than it cost—since a home is regarded as a means of future profit as well as a place in which to live.

With the Moon in Aquarius in the ninth house, the national income and much of the financial outlay is connected with countries distant from the United States. Much money is spent on foreign travel and for college education (also a ninth house matter), though the lack of adequate facilities in the lower grades and primary schools (fifth house) is one of the nation's real problems. On the whole, the people of the United States seek education for increased income (a typical Gemini attitude) rather than for the satisfaction to be gained through a greater knowledge of science, literature, art, or philosophy. The lack of men of college age planning extensive careers in any of these fields is marked. It is difficult to lure college students into these little-sought fields of culture because, compared to the commercial technical and scientific fields, the financial reward is limited.

With Mercury in Cancer and the Moon, its dispositor, in Aquarius, the American mind is inventive, as shown by the many commercial gadgets produced by our inventors. With Mars in Gemini in the national chart, and in fortunate aspect to the Moon, Americans are not without a superficial knowledge of many things little known to men of other lands. But the Gemini desire is to earn rather than learn, and this prevents the average man from digging deeply into any matter in which there is little profit.

The mercurial desire for a change of scene causes shifts in population that are inconceivable to European workers and others who think twice before leaving the family home or birthplace for no reason other than to add a few dollars to the income.

The reading habits of the nation are typically of Mercury–many newspapers and periodicals purchased with no great desire to read or study subjects which take time and require mental concentration. Many things temporarily occupy the attention of the average citizen, but few things on which he concentrates to the exclusion of all else.

Mercury in Cancer and the Moon in Aquarius make the average American subject to mental changes resulting in nationwide fads overnight, fads which come into being with Uranian suddenness and terminate just as quickly. The favorable trine of Mars to the Moon in Aquarius enables the average American to earn more than other men in a considerable variety of trades and professions. Consequently, the nature of the Gemini to profit by what he learns through higher forms of education is put to fortunate use by the Gemini-ruled population.

Compared to Capricorn-ruled India, the United States is a nation of youthful minds and youthful ideas. Far more value is put on practical knowledge than on spiritual truth or profound studies. Most Americans have little interest in any subject which does not put an extra dollar in the pocket. This results in a nation rich in profitable knowledge, but sadly lacking in the philosophical or occult truth needed for the growth of the soul.

Mercury is associated with the immature mind of

the post-adolescent. This is not high-quality thought, but thought which can be converted into immediate profit. It is the mental attitude of the average young man who looks for the quickest way to make as much income as possible. He does not want to spend months or years in any field to learn all there is to be known for the sake of knowledge itself. He seeks immediate returns for whatever knowledge he has, and often takes the first job to be found, rather than make further effort in preparation for potential future rewards.

The standard of the national judgment of success is to credit a man with having succeeded if he has made more money or made it faster than other men in his field. Americans do not value the discipline of the mind which brings its reward of truth only after long discipleship. Thus, as a nation, they are ill-conditioned to cope with nations comprised of men of a more mature type of mind who plan far ahead for long-term results.

This is a fault which, on a national scale, could prove America's greatest weakness. While as a nation Americans have plenty of practical know-how and great enthusiasm of rather brief duration, they lack discipline and stick-to-itiveness.

In this analysis of the national chart the nature of Mercury becomes clear. That nature is translated and modified by the sign Mercury occupies in the personal chart, coloring to the greatest possible degree the natural Mercury thought. If one has Mercury in a Saturn-ruled sign, the result will be a far more serious mind than if Mercury is in its natural sign, Gemini. If Mercury is in the Venus-sign Libra, it will take on the qualities of Venus thought, either highly spiritual or emotional, rather than the completely impersonal and practical mercurial thought of Gemini.

These are modifying qualities. The student should not be given to snap-judgment, therefore, nor to deciding by only the date of birth exactly what type of individual the chart represents. It is necessary to study the whole chart and arrive at a conclusion only after seeing the nature of the dispositor, its house position, and the aspects of every planet and every sign, and finally the ruler of every house.

There are few subjects in which one may find truth so tangible that it can be arrived at through tabulation. To know the true horoscope is to know truth, but truth is far too often distorted through the mind of the interpreter.

To all who ask, "Is there any truth to astrology?" the student should answer, "Astrology is as true as that upon which it is based—the very cosmic scheme itself." Yet when the medical profession first came into being, there were many physicians who prescribed the dangerously weakening bleeding of a patient, even to the point where sometimes the patient died from loss of blood. Does that compel one to think that there is nothing to the science of medicine? No. In that field of science the layman blames the practitioner's lack of knowledge for errors. Put the blame where it belongs when astrology is criticized—on the publicity-minded astrologer who insists on making irresponsible predictions.

Such predictions are a cancerous growth in the very body of the science itself.

This is not because predictions cannot be made correctly on the basis of astrology. But predictive interpretation in the nature of diagnostic judgment, based on a single factor and resting on limited knowledge, may in many cases be dangerous, even when such judgment is made by a physician. When a patient falls ill of a little-known ailment, few physicians do what the average astrologer is perfectly willing to do—put his opinion of the whole situation and its results on record without first consulting another fully qualified associate in his special field of knowledge.

This is the whole trouble with astrology. Far too many astrologers get themselves into print, desiring to gain the publicity which may bring them future profit, but are incompetent to predict the result of some impending event. Then when the event results, as sometimes happens, in a completely different way, astrology itself is all too often considered faulty. This conclusion is far from correct, but the predictive failure must be blamed primarily on the sort of interpretation the astrologer offers those who seek astrological judgment in print or in public gatherings.

The astrologer who steadfastly seeks truth must climb little by little to the pinnacle of knowledge. Far too many regard as adequate knowledge of astrology only the glimmerings of the profoundest, most soul-stirring and soul-searching revelation of God to be found within either oriental or occidental philosophy.

Actually astrology reveals even the nature of God through basic principles which are, more often than not, used only to attempt to foretell the course of man's little concerns.

Through knowledge of the quality of Neptune, man learns something of the all-pervasive influence of God as spirit. He may behold through the quality of Saturn, the discipline and denial put upon the self, or the Saturn-quality of God. In the Venus nature he learns the self-giving of God through physical expression and selfless love. Mercury, a part of the nature of God, is practical knowledge given to all men through experience, through which they acquaint themselves with the things necessary for functioning in mortal form. Jupiter is the benevolence of God, Mars the creative energy, Pluto the creative function.

Man knows so little compared to what may be known in time, through the esoteric knowledge of astrology, that the student should cease to think of astrology as a predictive way to gain attention or make personal profit and begin to learn, little by little, the very essence of truth.

18 Venus Selfless Love

Whatever is given for love, without desire for reward, rather than offered for profit or to add to personal advantage, is a gift which comes from the Omnipotent Source through the form-nature of Venus.

Allegorically, Venus was born from the Neptune-ruled sea. Neptune is spirit or the spirit-world. Therefore, Venus, emerging from the sea of spirit, presents beauty not born of the mortal world or created through the bounty of Jupiter. Venus is the freely-given-forth, selfless creation of what is beautiful. It may take many forms, many colors, many methods of creation.

Primarily it is what the artist expresses in beauty of color or shape. The true artist works to put into tangible form a spiritual awareness, which is in itself intangible. That form can only express, through some permanent medium, what the creator feels. Such artistic creation is not a result of the desire to make a large amount of money. Frequently the greatest artists have all but starved to be able to express in art or music what their souls demanded. They wrote, composed, painted, carved, or in some way put into fixed form their own particular awareness of truth. Venus truly expresses, therefore, the quality of substance born of the soul.

Venus is often mentioned, of course, in connection with the love of one mortal for another. But love, as man knows it, is of two forms. One comes from desire, and is ruled by Mars. This is love which creates, through the physical and sexual expression of desire, some physical form, or gratifies the self by complete possession of another. Transmuted or frustrated by circumstances or discipline, this desire may result in creations of a mental or emotional nature, but only when favorable aspects from Neptune turn it into desire to give of oneself.

Love, as expressed through Mars, is the quality of Omnipotence in mortal life making man desire to reproduce his own kind. Without desire, there would be few willing to assume the responsibilities of parenthood, or even assume responsibility for another's care.

The Venus-form of love derives from the spiritual nature of Omnipotence. Therefore, Venus indicates a desire to give of the self to create whatever is in the nature of Venus–beauty of thought, or form, harmony, grace, consideration for another, and the expression of spiritual awareness.

When Venus is conjunct a planet in any natal chart, this aspect indicates the selfless Venusian quality of a love directed toward whatever is suggested by the part of the birth chart ruled by the aspected planet.

Venus is not necessarily the planet that indicates possible marriage. Marriage is, in a sense, many-faceted. It is both a personal and business partnership, or, for some, a provision for a life of ease on the part of one or the other individual involved.

A progressed or transiting aspect to Venus in a natal chart should therefore be interpreted as indicating love which will benefit the native–love based on a giving of the self to the beloved rather than on a desire to possess the loved one or to profit from the association. One ought not, therefore, confuse what might be the material reasons for marriage with what results from an aspect of Venus. Many times marriage, even in America, is the expression of a far more practical attitude than the sacrifice of self for another, characteristic of Venus. More frequently it expresses the Martian quality of desire, the seeking to possess another sexually.

Many men desire women they do not love. Very few love those they do not desire. Many times, too, both men and women marry to produce, for the coming generation, offspring of their own creation. Europe is filled with such practical marital partnerships, in which love is of far less importance than a satisfactory personal relationship and a family. Such relationships usually survive far more successfully than marriage in America, where romantic love and sexual desire seem the primary motives.

Thus, fortunate aspects from Venus in the horoscope of one of marriageable age often do not result in marriage. A marriage may be made because of the need for Saturn's discipline in life or, as is seen in successful marriages (from the world's standpoint), Jupiter's aspect of material benefit. In some cases marriage results from the practical knowledge which is sought through association with another. The aspects from Mercury, not Venus, indicate this.

Only when a marriage shows a desire to give of self what another requires and accepts as love will Venus aspects indicate marriage rather than a romantic and freely given love which seeks no reward or return.

Neither does Venus always indicate romance, if one thinks of romance as sentiment. It may indicate that spiritual kind of love similar to ideal maternal love, which cherishes without seeking to possess or dominate. In every case, however, it indicates a love poured forth freely, directed at serving the loved one without thought of compensation. Therefore, such love has qualities of benevolence and goodness, but is seldom of a material nature—as in the case of a fortunate aspect of Jupiter—since many give greatly of love who are unable to give material proof of such devotion.

19 Mars The Desire Nature

The age-old concept that Mars, natural ruler of Aries, is also the ruler of the eighth house sign Scorpio came about through the association of Scorpio with death as well as with the physiological rulership of the excretory functions. The conversion of waste matter into new forms, such as fertilizer, logically belongs to Pluto, ruler of Scorpio. Yet one can see how Mars could become associated with Scorpio, for, as ruler of the first house (physical body), it creates new form, the beginning of finite life, through its rulership of the desire nature, which is a part of all creative effort. With Leo, the sign ruling the fifth house and the second of the fire trinity, desire gives form of a physical nature, whether children or great works of art, music or literature. Without desire nothing would come into being. In Sagittarius, ruler of the natural ninth house, desire is sublimated to stimulate the superconscious faculties of the mind and create, through contact with the Omnipotent Whole, greater concepts than mortal mind alone can conceive.

Because Scorpio was in past centuries said to be ruled

by "the negative side of Mars," the earliest astrologers thought that the functions of Scorpio were less positive, less vital to mortal evolution than those of Mars. From the physical standpoint, the Scorpio-ruled lower bowel, anus and the generative organs are normally considered essential to the continued health and functioning of adult individuals, yet in cases of cancer of these organs, certain artificial substitutes serve adequately for the elimination of waste matter from the body. Artificial impregnation of both human and animal life is not uncommon. We might therefore think that while Scorpio organs are considered important in a physical sense, they are not essential.

What Mars rules physically—the head—does not allow substitution and is therefore always essential to physical life, just as desire is always necessary for any type of creation.

Man feels the desire to mate sexually, with the result that the race is continued, whether or not either individual in the sexual union feels a need to reproduce life. Through desire for wealth and security, work is done which would seldom be performed if desire did not compel man to labor to produce income for either necessities or pleasures.

Desire to excel individually or as a member of some tribe, nation or group stimulates man to all forms of competition and war. Desire is the cardinal principle from which comes all effort, as the head is an essential physical entity without which life cannot exist.

The four points in the astrological chart ruled by the four cardinal signs in their natural order indicate this desire nature. The first, Aries, shows what is the most obvious desire of all life—to continue to function. This is the desire for life itself—the fear of death—the struggle to survive in spite of conditions which make life more hardship than opportunity.

The desire for a home is less fundamental, yet still one of man's reasons for working and giving up those freedoms which might interfere with his opportunity to maintain and enjoy exclusively the residence which is his castle. The home, ruled by Cancer, the second of the cardinal signs, often comes before marriage as one of the fundamental human desires.

The third cardinal sign, Libra, rules partnership and legal marriage. In view of the continued popularity of the wedded state, in spite of considerable discontent in individual cases, this can also be seen as one of the ways cardinal signs express the desire nature of the first house ruler.

The fourth cardinal sign in the natural horoscope—Capricorn—rules the tenth house. This is the desire for acclaim from the world, for recognition, for success above and beyond what others may attain. Without desire for such recognition, few would do what must be done to gain outstanding recognition. Many are crucified on this cardinal cross, for it is all but impossible to attain the full measure of satisfaction in all four fields ruled by the cardinal signs. Yet desire still prompts man to seek complete reward for his efforts in these four fields, though more often than not he must sacrifice a large measure of what might be gained in one in order to attain greater compensation in another.

The trines involving the Mars-ruled sign indicate what can be accomplished through desire. Other cardinal signs are in square or conflict with the first sign, Aries, but the trines are avenues of more rewarding expression of Mars. Through desire man may know the sexual satisfaction that comes through Leo, a fixed sign, and that is therefore expressed physically. Through this physical outlet, he also may give expression to desire in creating offspring, but desire finds expression in all forms of creation through the fifth house. In the transmuted expression of the desire nature, man may create mentally by contact with the Sagittarius-ruled higher mind—the superconscious faculty. However, if desire is continually satisfied on the physical level, no stimulus is left for such contact—the reason for emphasis on celibacy in those who seek to reach beyond the level of the ordinary mind.

The development of what starts with desire can be traced without difficulty through every division of the natural chart. Man desires to live (Aries), then to gain possessions (Taurus), then to make contact or communicate with those in his immediate environment (Gemini), The fundamental desire for his own home comes ahead of these secondary urges for most of humanity, since the fourth house in the natural chart is cardinal.

The normal growth of each individual comes through experience gained in the first six houses of the chart. But there are levels of accomplishment higher than those expressed through the houses of personal experience that are also the ultimate result of desire sublimated or transmuted. Regardless of how far desire carries the individual from the fundamental desire for life itself, desire is essentially a part of the individual pattern of being. The Aries symbol, the curved horns joined in a descending vertical line, shows the life force from Omnipotent Creative Source descending into the head or brain of mortal form. Aries, unlike those signs which hold upraised symbolic lines to plead for bounty from the Source, does not seek to hold this force, but to pour out the energy that the brain receives. It is a fire sign, and the characteristic of Mars is ceaseless activity.

Instead of acting entirely on the physical level, however, Mars conditions the house it rules to expression through continued and aggressive desire. In the third house or ruling it, Mars indicates that the mental activity and speech will be rapid—the desire for speedy expression stimulating Mercury's natural house. When Mars rules the fifth, the sexual desire will be greater than ordinary, but the aspects in the individual chart determine how this desire will be expressed.

One sexually afflicted chart has the four cardinal signs all occupied by malefic planets, with Mars in the Venus-ruled sign Libra, Uranus in the Mars-ruled Aries, Pluto in Moon-ruled Cancer and Saturn in close unfortunate aspect to these three malefics, in Capricorn. This is the chart of a man who admitted that his abnormal sexual desire (Uranus in Aries) had cause him to commit innumerable rapes and finally to kill violently and sadistically thirteen women. This may show the frightening nature of Mars when afflicted, without either control or sublimation to divert the desire-nature into constructive channels.

Since violence, the unpremeditated action of Mars when destructively used, is consistent with the nature of war, Mars was given jurisdiction over contests requiring violent action on the part of the individuals rather than prolonged or continued programs of destruction. When slower moving planets are in aspect to natal planets or planets in the chart of a nation, the transits of Mars explode and touch off the outbreak of action, even when long-range plans have been made for the final step. The symbol of Mars, like that of Aries, suggests the creation of matter or form resulting from solar activity. Hence Mars rules the sexual desire through which new life comes into being. While Mars would naturally have been given rulership over death, an eighth house function, during ages when death more often than not resulted from violence, the whole nature of this planet is so opposed to Pluto's function that it must be seen as energy, desire and action rather than the destruction of outmoded form by physical termination of the life, unless such life terminates by accident or fire, both under the rulership of Mars.

20 Jupiter Principle of Expansion

Man gropes through many forms of religious thought in search of truth. The past, better than the present, gives a clearer picture of his evolving concept of good or what he calls God, the benefactor. He first worshipped fire, because it gave him superiority over the beasts of the jungle in a time when life depended on skill as much as courage and strength.

But fire and the metals fire forged into spears and hunting knives are under the planetary rulership of Mars, not Jupiter. Therefore, God, in man's earliest thought, was a god of war, a god of cruelty, a god of destruction. Mars rules all these things. But a god conceived as one who aids in the fury of battle to destroy the enemy, who gives fire to make weapons which kill other forms of life and men of other tribes, fell short of the concept early man had of the principle of good.

With a Mars-type god, goodness was courage and generosity in making sacrifice before battle (if such sacrifice brought defeat to the enemy) and before the hunt when divine aid was sought in killing more and more creatures for food and skins. While this conception was useful, since it provided prehistoric man with what he desired, a god limited to assisting in the slaughter of other men and lesser creatures would find few worshippers when men prayed for peace on earth. At the stage of growth at which man found himself when he believed that God demanded living sacrifice, however, this idea was reasonable. The changing concepts of God through the history of man's development show that He is conceived in each period as a deity who assists and answers the mortal needs felt by men of that period.

In the age when men worshipped the Sun, they saw the Sun as good because it brought growth of plant life, and plant life was essential for man to live through periods of famine or lack of game. Therefore, the Sun became a concept of God to be worshipped.

In the period of the old civilization of Greece, Zeus (Jupiter to the Romans) was considered the greatest of many gods, because men were not yet able to conceive of the attributes of all their gods incorporated in a single supreme being. Jupiter represented the principle of growth. Because increase and growth were good, Jupiter became, and still remains, a symbol of benefit, good fortune, luck, gain, expansion, and blessing. Only the few who have no need for growth of any kind feel no need for the Jupiter concept of a god "from whom all blessings flow."

Not only does man desire to grow and progress, but all nature provides this pattern of compelled growth. Therefore, in all aspects of the planet Jupiter, the student of astrology, like the ancient Greeks, see Jupiter as the beneficent god, the planet which gives all and asks little in return–or so it seems.

While man comes, through eons of time, to think of the attributes of God as akin to those of the planets which are nearer to the center of his universe, the present pattern of deity rests on a combined concept of the nature of the greatest of the Greek and Roman gods, Zeus/Jupiter, and the practical Taurean earth, which represents fundamentally all things of a material nature.

But to think of God in terms of the nature of Jupiter is an error if such a god is believed to give unearned luck or benefit. The law of karma is fundamental truth. Therefore, "As ye give, so shall ye receive" was taught by the Master Jesus. What is given out to benefit another, in any form, is returned from the reservoir of good that man calls God, as surely as planting seed produces rewarding crops.

The house position of Jupiter in every birth chart shows the part of the life in which each individual gains the reward of the good he has given in this or any previous life.

Jupiter, interpreted astrologically, gives increase and growth of body, mind, or soul. Therefore, man gains, in periods of favorable Jupiter aspects to planets in the natal chart, both in physical growth and material substance, as well as in mental development. According to past conduct, he receives the rewards that result from a favorable transit of Jupiter, and claims the good fortune promised by the position of Jupiter in the birth chart. If he achieves ever-increasing growth, this achievement shows that in some past time he put forth for others the same quality and quantity of good. Jupiter is not luck, but the principle of benefit resulting from the expression of benevolence toward another. If a man ever denies to others the help they seek, he denies to himself, in the future, this same help, and may reincarnate with an unfavorable, or badly aspected Jupiter in his birth chart to indicate that denial.

Because Jupiter manifests itself as growth along all lines, many think that it indicates luck more than deserved reward. This same viewpoint probably sees Saturn as undeserved discipline or denial, since it takes no account of karmic law.

Transits of Jupiter

While the quality of growth resulting from a transiting or progressed aspect of Jupiter is indicated by the nature of the sign in which Jupiter may be at that time, the quantity, or the amount of the resulting growth or gain, must be determined by the duration of the aspect.

If in the natal chart there are planets so placed in sequence or trine that one after another gets the effect of this favorable influence, the individual will have longer or greater periods of good fortune without interruption than he would if he only enjoyed the transiting aspect of Jupiter over a single planet. What happens in the life of the individual with several planets aspected in succession might be compared to a long growing season in nature, with the result that substantial crops are produced and reach maturity. The transit over a single planet gives a period of bright sunshine and favorable conditions too brief to produce more than a limited return.

Thus a sequence of favorable aspects is even better than the result of a grand trine in which all planets are aspected fortunately at the same time, for while this well-aspected trine gives more than ordinary luck during the transiting aspect, the duration of such a condition is necessarily shorter.

The nature of benefits resulting from a Jupiter aspect, if the aspect is the trine, conjunction, or sextile–all fortunate–does not, however, make this time of good fortune always one when great amounts of money are made, in spite of the fact that the symbol for Jupiter is the curved Moon, symbol of the self, above (and thus overcoming) the cross of material curcumstances.

If the transit takes place in one of the four cardinal signs–Aries, Cancer, Libra, or Capricorn–the benefit results because the individual is coming into a period of spiritual growth stimulated by Jupiter in one of the signs which rules the eternal spirit. If the aspect is a conjunction, Jupiter in a spiritual sign will of course bring growth to the spirit itself; therefore, the results are not likely to increase the fortune or material possessions–unless Jupiter also forms a trine or sextile to a planet in a fixed sign. Spiritual growth is an inner experience often unnoticed by others.

If, through such an experience during the Jupiter transit, the practical mind is stimulated to greater growth, inspired through inner illumination, it is thus able to produce mental work of a finer quality than is accomplished under other circumstances. If the planet receiving the stimulation of Jupiter's trine aspect is in a fixed sign, actual material benefit may result, stimulated by inner attitudes of greater confidence. This is the sort of lucky aspect which might bring reward for some former deed done without thought of personal gain, or repayment in cash for spiritual inspired creative work.

When Jupiter transits through one of the fixed signs—Taurus, Leo, Scorpio, or Aquarius—what results in the way of expanded benefits must come from a material source. The benefit may accrue to the pocketbook, the mind, or the spirit, depending on the nature of the sign in which the planet aspected by Jupiter is placed.

Jupiter in a fixed sign, transiting over a planet in a fixed sign, will result in growth, luck, or good fortune along material lines. This will happen every twelve years to those who have their natal Jupiter in a fixed sign, for it takes that long for Jupiter to return to its natal position.

Every fortunate aspect of Jupiter, however, does not bring increased income through little effort. Transiting planets, as well as natal planets, function *always* in accordance with the quality of the sign in which they are placed at birth, or in which they are transiting or in progressed aspect.

Those who have Jupiter in a fixed sign at birth, particularly if it is favorably aspected, may be considered more fortunate in a material way than others, if not more intelligent or finer in spirit, since every four years their natal Jupiter is favorably aspected from either a fixed, mutable, or cardinal sign, bringing periods when some fortunate circumstance develops to give a new spurt of material growth. The initial aspect may mark the first development in some professional line, which will, in the whole twelve years of Jupiter's full transit of the birth chart, reach the point of public acceptance and recognition. A Jupiter aspect may coincide with repeated periods of better income from the house natal Jupiter occupies.

Should natal Jupiter be in a fixed sign, but in an adverse square aspect to other natal planets, there is conflict or challenge shown. Under favorable Jupiter transits, the individual attempts to expand, but must constantly feel the limitation put on him by the house in the natal chart which contains the square. The effect of an opposition is to pull the native away from the goal he seeks, and growth must be made in spite of a handicap. Therefore, he is less likely to reach the degree of perfection he would if there were no restrictions or difficulties to hold back what Jupiter stimulates to greater fullness.

When transiting Jupiter is in conjunction, trine or sextile to those planets which obstruct or limit the benefit promised by the natal Jupiter, there is temporarily an expansion of benefits. For as transiting Jupiter moves around the natal chart at the rate of approximately one sign a year, it is like sunshine falling on that particular spot in the garden. Whatever is growing there is stimulated and increases, offering good return and benefit more than at other times.

One should concentrate on the part of the chart favorably aspected by Jupiter to achieve as much growth as possible in connection with the matters with which the house is concerned.

When some houses of the chart are under favorable or discouraging aspects from other planets, however, it is consoling to think that in a few years there must be a fortunate aspect to that troublesome part of life from luck-giving Jupiter. Therefore, the matters ruled by that house should never be viewed without considering some possibility of improvement, for when Jupiter transits any house of the horoscope, it increases the quality or quantity of substance or condition indicated by that house for the whole period of the transit, and fosters a "growing season" in that special part of life.

It must always be remembered, however, that one transiting aspect does not determine the complete situation or condition. In considering a single aspect operating at any time, first judge it in relation to the time it will continue to be within orb of the aspected natal planet, as compared to the time during which some other planet, possibly of contrasting nature, will be aspecting the same or another planet in the birth chart.

The slower transits of the more distant planets—Pluto, Neptune, Uranus, and Saturn—are of greater importance in their effect, not only because of their own nature, but also because of the length of time they require to complete the transit, compared with the fortunate but briefer effect of Jupiter. Conditions at a time when both favorable Jupiter and adverse Pluto aspects exist, for example, may reflect more Pluto's destruction of old conditions (assuming that Pluto is in conjunction or adverse aspect) than the benefits of Jupiter. Such combined aspects are like a sunny day in midwinter—the hours during which the Sun shines seem brighter and less unpleasant than hours of darkness and cold, but their duration is limited and the conditions of winter brought about by more slowly moving planets in adverse aspect endure after the Sun ceases to shine.

The period of the Jupiter transit is a break in the clouds and therefore welcome, but the student must not be too quick to promise complete and lucky changes of circumstances simply because there is a Jupiter transit impending. The ability to weigh and balance the effect of all transits at any time comes only after years of practice and experience, but it must be developed if one is not to be too reassuring or discouraging in appraising future conditions.

Assuming, however, that only the fortunate transit of Jupiter is aspecting a particular part of the horoscope, or a planet under consideration (which is seldom the case), the student may look for some form of expansion or gain at that time in connection with whatever matters are ruled by the house transited and the house ruled by any planet favorably aspected by the benefic.

Jupiter in the First House

Taking the first house of the chart, for example, with Jupiter transiting through a fixed sign therein, one may expect increase in weight or faster growth for those not completely mature, since Jupiter in fixed signs makes all material form increase. This is the weight-watcher's warning! If the transit by conjunction happens to be in a mutable sign, greater mental development becomes apparent and the mind is stimulated. But if the transit is in a cardinal sign, the only change seen in the personality is greater growth of spirit and a more benevolent and Jupiter-like attitude in relation to the conditions of life. A philosophical point of view will come about during such a transit, and an "all's well with the world" feeling, even though no changes of circumstances account for this constructive viewpoint.

This same rule holds true if the favorable aspect of transiting Jupiter is to the planet ruling the ascendant, and the nature of quality of that planet will determine how the effect will show in the personality. Weight-watchers might, therefore, dread a transit of Jupiter over the first house ruler if it is a fixed sign; if the ruler is in a cardinal or mutable sign, the individual seeking philosophical growth or intellectual expansion will see a period greatly to be desired. Physically, the transit brings better-than-average health and good spirits to assist the assimilation of food.

Jupiter in the Second House

Though the second house is one of material possessions, a Jupiter transit through it or over its ruler is no assurance of increased income unless the ruler of the second is in a fixed sign. If the ruler is in a mutable sign, the transit may bring the good fortune to pick up a fine literary collection for very little cost or to receive as gifts valuable books, through which mental growth will be stimulated. If the second house is ruled by a mutable sign, many literary treasures will be collected and prized, and more than the usual amount of money (in relation to other expenditures) will be spent for books or study courses. The individual accumulates treasures for the mind rather than things of monetary nature, or earns income by some mental activity if a mutable sign rules the second house.

If the second house is ruled by a cardinal sign, there is seeming indifference to accumulating material things or striving hard to increase income. The transit of a cardinal second house truly marks the individual who is "laying up treasures in heaven" or who is completely lacking in desire to increase his share of this world's goods. Ministers might be expected to show this house rulership many times, and those whom the world regards as ill-paid may feel rich in spite of lack of financial rewards.

When Saturn rules this second house, we see the effect of a cardinal (spiritual) sign on what is, in the natural birth chart, ruled by the fixed sign Taurus. But should Saturn ruling this house be in trine to some important planet in a fixed sign, the individual will gain wealth and retain it in spite of little desire for material things. Those who put a low value on accumulation of many things often find that unsought benefits accrue to them under this transiting aspect.

Adverse aspects of transiting Jupiter or natal adverse aspects to this planet of expansion reflect themselves in overexpansion, overbuying, overdoing–overloading the life with so many things that they constitute a burden to care for, insure, house, and clean. The typical collector of great amounts of anything is likely to have such a natal aspect, making desire for possessions far exceed need. This is a particularly unfortunate aspect for one responsible for purchasing a home or business, for the result is always overbuying, waste, and loss. This indeed could be called "too much of a good thing."

Jupiter in the Third House

Transits over the ruler of the third house, or through it, can increase practical knowledge, bring pleasant or profitable trips in nearby communities, bring benefit from neighbors or from improvements in the immediate neighborhood of the home or present living quarters, and make the mind less inclined toward serious thought or worry over practical problems. To those with brothers or sisters this transit may give benefit from one or the other.

Jupiter in the Fourth House

Because the fourth house shows conditions at the end of life, and land, property and home affairs, these matters show improvement and more prosperous or fortunate conditions when Jupiter is in that part of the chart, or favorably aspecting the ruler of this house.

Jupiter in the Fifth House

Jupiter transiting or favorably aspecting the planet ruling the fifth house may bring romance with a fairly wealthy or socially prominent individual. For those who have children, this is a period when happiness, benefit, and good fortune will come through them, or honor will come to them reflecting credit upon the parent.

For those with fortunate aspects for speculation in the chart (and *only* for those), this transit of the fifth house marks the most favorable time to take chances on the market or in any form of speculation, if other aspects are also favorable. Persons connected with the theatre, motion pictures, or concert stage will find this time favorable for their ventures. Since the fifth house is also one of creative thought, transits in favorable aspect through it or to its ruler correspond with original ideas of real value or creations in art, music, or poetry which will prove successful.

Jupiter in the Sixth House

Jupiter transiting or favorably aspecting the sixth house marks the time when those who rent property will get a satisfactory tenant in it. Employees engaged under this aspect will give fine service and prove of great benefit through their work. Better health should be enjoyed, even by those not always in the best condition physically. Small animals owned or purchased at this time will give more pleasure than problems, and some very fine pet may be acquired under a Jupiter transit of the sixth house.

Jupiter in the Seventh House

If progressed and other transiting aspects are similar in nature, the Jupiter transit through the seventh house or Jupiter's favorable aspects to the ruler of this house, give the best opportunities for a fortunate marriage or legal partnership. Those already married find the marriage a greater source of good fortune now than in other years. This is also the best time for making public appearances, for on such occasions the individual gains increased prestige and popularity. Regardless of how little response the public may show during other periods, during transits of Jupiter through the seventh there is a warm response from the audience and more appreciation of whatever is offered.

Jupiter in the Eighth House

The eighth house, ruling the money or possessions of the marriage or business partner, brings increased benefit from this source when Jupiter transits it. Where some existing condition comes to an end during this transit, the termination brings more benefit than loss. Even when life ends under a favorable transit of Jupiter, if other aspects agree, dying will be the peaceful release from suffering which all desire.

Jupiter in the Ninth House

Jupiter's transit through the ninth house is the time when, if necessary, legal action should be started and legal matters put before the court. It is also a period of growth along religious and philosophical lines. If, in the birth chart, Jupiter is unfavorably aspected, however, whatever benefit results from action taken at such time will be limited. Where the birth chart shows unfavorable aspects to Jupiter, it is wise to avoid, if possible, all legal action, since natal aspects always overshadow the influence of transits. But if such action cannot be avoided, it should be started in the period when, if ever, the law will be favorable. While the action may still prove costly and troublesome, the opponent will be less determined and the court more lenient than at other times.

Jupiter in the Tenth House

Reputation which outlasts income, work and even life is shown in the tenth house. If this house is fortunate by aspect or holds some luck-bringing planet, the transit of

Jupiter through it will be a time when the professional or personal reputation gains in importance in the eyes of the world. Through other periods more work may be done, more appreciation merited, but until Jupiter transits the tenth house, one may work hard for success yet never gain acclaim. Actually through each transit of Jupiter in favorable aspect to this house, some gain is made, but the tenth house shows how one is remembered by the world, since final judgment often does not come until after death.

Frequently individuals are best known for something which was not the life work nor profession, but some exploit or adventure or creation which brought the personality into the spotlight, to gain a reputation out of all proportion to the effort made to attain it. Many composers and artists denied income and honor in their lifetime are acclaimed genuine masters of their art years after death, if their tenth house has fortunate aspects.

Where there are adverse aspects to the ruler of the tenth house by planets which rule other houses, recognition and reputation, even if better than average, will suffer to the extent that the conditions of the houses involved cause criticism or in some way detract from the prestige attained. Also, adverse aspects from more slowly moving planets can overshadow and diminish Jupiter's beneficial influence.

Even when Jupiter is favorably aspected, however, it is important to take advantage of the favorable condition rather than sit and wait for luck to fall in one's lap. When Jupiter is transiting the tenth house, it is time to expand the professional field of operation and make contacts in line with the growth desired. More failures than one realizes are caused by letting fortunate aspects pass without seeking to get the utmost benefit from them. Jupiter's aspects may bring good conditions on a small scale if, at the time they form, one is content to pass the fortunate time in a limited field of operation. To utilize this period of luck fully the wise man or woman will prepare for all expansion possible through the whole period of Jupiter's transit, only ceasing to push their luck when the aspect is past. Since the tenth house rules the reputation of the individual, this period is one in which loftier ambition may be expressed. It is the time when both the soul and the self feel the need of "more stately mansions." Through each Jupiter transit some amount of growth is made. As in nature, what was added to the stature does not shrink in value, though it may seem to remain dormant for some time. But the results of twelve years of growth, even if such growth is intermittent, are much more obvious than that achieved during a single Jupiter aspect. Therefore, each aspect of this planet builds up into greater form or expression whatever accomplishment is indicated by the planet aspected.

Jupiter in the Eleventh House

When Jupiter transits or favorably aspects the eleventh house, friends may prove of benefit financially, mentally, or spiritually, according to the quality of the sign Jupiter occupies. Income from profession increases, and if advice is sought, those who advise will assist progress. The circle of friends may include someone of considerable wealth or importance, and relations with friends will prove a source of personal opportunity and good fortune.

Jupiter in the Twelfth House

The twelfth house is astrologically considered a place of seclusion and either voluntary confinement or restriction through illness or the law. But when Jupiter transits this house, even such enforced restriction and seclusion are benefits and may provide protection against something much less fortunate. Confinement in institutions and hospitals is less unpleasant during such periods, and all work done out of contact with the public will go well. Since the twelfth house is also the house indicating the karmic debt, the transit of Jupiter through this house is the time when one may repay (as a result of what Jupiter brings in luck, money or knowledge) some of the obligations indicated by the planets in this house.

The twelfth house, indicating secret enemies rather than those who oppose the individual openly, as signified in the seventh house, is not benefited by the Jupiter transit, however, since it may bring into the life someone who is important or legally qualified to place added restriction upon one during the period of this transit. This, though, must be seen as the karmic result of what the soul still in training through repeated incarnations has done to another in some past life, for under such restriction one pays off a debt and balances the books, so that in a future incarnation there will be no need of such restitution.

In estimating the results of any transit of Jupiter, remember that this is the planet of expansion and growth if well-aspected or unaspected, but its adverse aspects in the natal chart, and by transit, may cause one to suffer through overexpansion on what ever level of growth results from the Jupiter transit.

21
Saturn
Life's Discipline

Saturn's effect on the life of the individual is not in any sense that of a destroyer.

Saturn disciplines. It increases substance through depriving man of what is unnecessary, but in that way augments things that are of true importance, by delivering strength to certain forces integrated in the chart instead of permitting them to be scattered broadcast and wasted. Therefore, it is important to see the effect resulting from the transit of Saturn through the chart as the improved quality of the self.

The soul incarnates on earth in order to attain, in continuous periods of experience, those truths that may be gained only through experience. Therefore, Saturn's transits are periods of the soul's search for more physical experience. Through them it seeks to grow–not through thought, or through inner awareness, but through living and getting to the very highest point by a supreme effort of the self.

Saturn disciplines the self by putting on it the burden of the soul. It brings to bear on the physical being a certain well-recognized feeling of the soul's dissatisfaction, which causes the self to take inventory of what it has accomplished.

The self is made aware of the soul's thought, that though the self has what it wants and what it considers necessary, it has not attained the soul's desire. At such a time, man realizes that he has gained something which he thought important, but at the same time he is aware that he has lost what he set out to gain in the first place. This may seem illogical unless one realizes that what all men truly seek is satisfaction of soul, even beyond satisfaction of material ambitions.

Contrary and at cross-purposes to this inner desire, however, man puts himself to the task of securing what the self desires through material success. When he first comes into the mortal world, he thinks that he desires things, of many kinds–luxuries, money, property–the symbols of success. With the idea that these things bring happiness, he makes a determined effort to secure them. Yet when he eventually attains what he desired, he has only an awareness of an added burden put upon him by the property he accumulated and the possessions he prized, and by the very degree of success he attained.

This is Saturn's way to descipline. It places in the hands of the willful child what he seeks, but since he desires it only until it is fully in his possession, he soon finds it no longer gives satisfaction. In gaining what seemed to be most desireàble to the self, the soul assumes the burden it must bear. The soul creates desire for possessions for the self, but, when the individual has gained these things, the soul is completely unsatisfied.

So under Saturn's transits a man has the futile and defeated feeling that though he found what he wanted, there is something still lacking. For the most part, the only results are many additional responsibilities.

In this way man discovers truth through experience. He is not told that he will not find happiness through gaining all the things he desires. He is not taken to a point, as in the story of the temptation of the Master Jesus, from which he might survey the kingdoms of the earth and be permitted to choose between worldly symbols of power and success and the Kingdom of Heaven. Man's soul enters mortal life to bring him in contact with the material possessions, to see them as greatly desirable from the distant viewpoint. Only by having attained them does he fail to find them satisfying. Then he may begin to think that it is what the soul seeks which is truly worth having, since he has found nothing else which satisfies his real desire.

Thus Saturn, like Satan, is the tempter, since he gives all men the thought that what the self desires must be considered most important to happiness and satisfaction. It is only by this that men are led to put forth their efforts and to learn through experience that possessions fail to satisfy the soul. In this way only can the self become aware of the true need of the soul.

The self is so unaware that many times those who know the dissatisfaction which ferments during periods of Saturn transits, do not realize why they feel as they do. They cannot understand their discontent. From the standpoint of material things they have far more than they ever expected to possess. But they have become aware of the soul's desire, for it is the soul that material treasure leaves unsatisfied. Only through seeking spiritual treasures can it know attainment and satisfaction.

Saturn is, therefore, both the tempter and the disciplinarian, and, in a sense, the celestial teacher of what the soul requires. The soul desires truth, and through seeking truth, delivers the self from Saturn's discipline for considerable periods of time. Between those periods of discipline, the self dominates to the extent that it accumulates chiefly things of a material nature, and, for the time, feels that through such accumulation success has been attained.

But every seventh year, Saturn aspects the Sun in the personal chart, letting the self become aware of lack of satisfaction.

Saturn is the principle of denial of desire. Desire is the pinnacle of perfected happiness. With desire the whole process of growth begins. Without desire, man is like the sloth, the snail, the growth upon the stone, with no incentive for accomplishment other than to settle in one spot and stay there. Unless a man desires something, he has no urge to do anything to attain what he wants. Desire is the point at which the self puts forth the first effort, and in the *process* of growth, it gains greater and ever greater happiness, since it becomes aware, in the development which comes with the accomplishment, of the opportunities for further expansion and the benefits which result from effort.

But when the self accomplishes what it desires, desire

ceases. Without desire, what is there? So Saturn benefits humankind by providing restrictions of present opportunity and creating a period in which new desires develop.

In the Orient it is thought that the man who knows no desires is fortunate, but fortunate in what sense? Only because his soul feels satisfied. The soul so rich in spiritual worth that it does not desire material things is a soul free of the bondage of the self. But how few such souls can be found!

Saturn, however, disciplines the self through the soul by internal rather than external action. During Saturn transits the soul's disappointment in what the self has accomplished is felt in periodical surveys of the self's progress. Between these periods, the self is permitted to think that what it has accumulated is still far from adequate.

Discipline in other forms is also put on the self many times by other planetary transits. Uranus brings termination by exterior changes about which the self has little to say. It is put to the test of having to accept some catastrophic circumstance without seeing the necessity or reason for what comes to pass.

Neptune, though long delayed in action, really gives the same sort of result. In the way termites slowly and secretly do away with the substantial foundations of even the strongest structure, Neptune secretly undermines things which seem so permanent and well-settled. These transits and their effects are no less detrimental to the self than Saturn's discipline. They cause far more destruction of what exists through the efforts of the individual, or in the circumstances in his life, than Saturn's trivial pruning back of too-profuse growth.

Man looks on Uranian upsets with shock and bewilderment, seeing his life so completely changed overnight. But with Saturn aspects there is something of sadness and disappointment, for he realizes that in spite of all that has been gained or accomplished, there is still no satisfaction.

He feels this way because the soul is speaking through the self, and sees self-ambition as so futile and time-wasting. Saturn, therefore, reveals the soul's yearning for what is truly worth having in contrast to the self's desire, which seeks what is needed to satisfy the self only.

The sense of discontent ought not to be felt by those who have developed the soul to a point where they become aware of that lack of full satisfaction, in spite of material success. But for those who regard the self as paramount over all else, and for all purposes superior, these transits of Saturn are essential to make the self realize that there is within each man some superconscious awareness that all is not well.

Those who ask, "Why am I so ill-pleased with what I have, when I am far better off than I was, and so fortunate in relation to many others?" have a soul developed to the point where it makes the self understand the soul's purpose and likewise its disappointment in what the self has accomplished. The individual who feels this should realize that in him the soul manifests itself clearly. He is made to understand that the pile upon pile of worldly goods in his store are only impediments to his spiritual progress.

22 Uranus The Creative Will

Uranus is the most revolutionary of all the planets in the solar system. This rebelliousness is also the fundamental quality of Uranian thought and of all forms of Uranian activity. Those who are strongly affected by the influence of Uranus are counteractive. They do not simply stop or impede action, but often completely reverse it. Not only do Uranian thought and will oppose the thought and will of those ruled by other planets, they seek also to change the courses of action of those people. Therefore the Uranian person acts contrary to well-established precedent and in opposition to many conventional opinions or forms of conduct.

This is because Uranus manifests the creative will of the supercreative Source, the power behind all creation. The function of this planet is to unite form with Superform and thus become the instrument by which Superior Will or Omnipotent Intelligence is made manifest to man.

Uranus may be best understood if the student thinks in terms of an analogy. Consider electric power as it functions in radio, television, the light bulb, and the coils and wires of the electric stove or heater. Electricity itself is unobserved; its effects, however, are obvious.

A similar situation exists in the cosmic picture. By what Uranus does, man becomes aware of its nature and quality. Its effects may be observed in the lightning and electrical energy in earth's atmosphere; but apart from these indications of its power, Uranus is intangible and invisible.

Yet Uranus exerts a magnetic force so tremendous that it sparks all activity in the cosmos. Its function may be illustrated again by analogy; think of a spark which ignites gas vapor. Until it is ignited, such vapor is of no value in supplying energy.

In the same way Neptune, representing thought from the Superior Mind, is not made manifest until Uranus, symbolizing the Superconscious Will, activates Neptune's intangible quality, making man aware of its power. Astrologers therefore teach that Uranus rules man's superconscious mental capacity.

This is the level of thought that is attained through Jupiter's beneficent quality, expressed through the so-called higher mind or inspiration. It is not the type of thought man gains through Mercury, ruler of the conscious mind; for the conscious mind gains knowledge from reading, listening and direct experience. Neither is it the vague and diffused, intuitive Neptune-related thought, which so seldom makes any impression at all on one who is attuned to Neptune's transits.

Uranus' is thought energy—energy making itself manifest through thought, stimulating man's mind by inspiring him with new and original ideas, inventions, drastic opinions and revolutionary concepts. Hence, under the influence of aspects of Uranus, man is mentally more strongly urged to act than at any other time.

Mars also stimulates action—by energizing man; but the energy of Mars is best expressed through muscular coordination and through the practical mind or the emotional nature. Many planets exert vibrations or create force in a definite direction, causing the mind and emotions to be active, depressed or optimistic according to the nature of each aspecting planet. Through Uranus alone the mental and spiritual qualities of Neptune reach man's awareness.

Uranus also reveals its nature through the kind of energy it develops in forms other than mortal minds. This nature is seen in the lightning bolt ripping through the clouded sky. The lightning is not Uranian itself, but contains Uranian force directed against cosmic vapors or clouds. Frequently, this same force is heard but not seen if thunder, not lightning, heralds an approaching storm. It may be said, therefore, that Uranus' existence may be confirmed when man notes the force it exerts. When the planet is operating thus, the senses of man are made aware of something unusual and unexpected disrupting the ordinary environment.

The astrologer is better able to predict changes of an unforeseen nature when Uranus forms aspects to any planet in the natal chart than when other planetary aspects form, for the action of Uranus is always radical, out of the ordinary, and surprising—in the cosmos as well as in the life of the individual.

Like the lightning flash, the changes Uranus brings come suddenly and from no apparent source—often from one which seemed most unlikely to cause such upsets. Therefore, the astrologer, seeking to predict what will happen under an aspect of Uranus to a given planet, might be much wiser to limit predictions to "Expect the unexpected. Neither the best that you hope for nor the worst that you fear will come to pass, but something completely unexpected will happen."

One may, of course, determine that part of life which will feel the effect of the sudden change or new development by observing the house of the birth chart ruled by Uranus and the point where this planet is transiting at the time the aspect forms. Both the Uranus-ruled house and the part of the chart aspected by the Uranus transit will combine to create the condition, while the effect will be felt in that part of the chart ruled by the natal planet aspected.

To many, unexpected action is more terrifying than either Neptune's adverse wasting-away influence or Saturn's delays and discipline. It is an unwelcome visitation to mortals who prefer to keep whatever they have accumulated and remain in whatever fortunate situation has been attained. Therefore, the fact that Uranus wipes out, as do Uranus-ruled earthquakes, some present condition or situation, gives it a malefic connotation to those who find present conditions preferable to change.

What logical reason can astrology give for such forced change in man's life pattern? Man deplores the loss of his security. If he feels well-established, he has no desire for further experience that might cost him present positive opportunities. Uranus, however, forms some disruptive aspect to every natal planet about every twenty-one years, compelling individuals to develop in new directions characteristics that the aspected natal planet rules—whether these changes are desired or not. Without such change and the new experience that follows, the soul cannot continue its growth through finite experience.

Uranian changes are not, of course, always changes of circumstance. As is true for those caused by the aspects of other planets, the nature of such changes depends upon the type of sign in which the transited or aspected planet is located. Even a complete change of inner nature, such as Uranus can cause if in square or opposition to a planet in a cardinal sign, may not be observable to outsiders, though it is deeply felt by the person subjected to Uranus' influence. Neither is it likely that the adverse aspect of Uranus to a planet in a mutable sign will do more than cause a sudden change of mental attitude in connection with the matter ruled by the natal planet aspected, though from such complete changes of mind changes of condition often develop. It must be seen, too, that the conjunction of Uranus to a planet in one of the fixed signs must form a fortunate trine to planets in mutable or cardinal signs close to the same degree as the aspected conjunction; therefore, in some charts it is possible for the conjunction to be a very fortunate aspect.

When a chart shows a trine or sextile aspect from this planet of the unexpected, some situation or opportunity may come to pass without advance planning, yet spectacularly bringing sudden success. In these instances, Uranus seems to open a new door to fulfillment of desire in a most unlikely way. Such fortunate trines form to natal planets approximately every twenty-eight years, and new opportunities coming at such times could be of the utmost importance.

Just the reverse is true of the results of matters started under the square or opposition of Uranus. Such opportunities, while they may seem to promise much, often turn out to be no more than somewhat bitter experiences. Astrologers ought to point out at all times the probability that whatever path is taken under an adverse Uranus aspect will prove a dead-end road. However, man is so impelled by the force of Uranus that, in spite of such admonitions and the experience of others, he is more likely to take this *seemingly* fine opportunity than remain in whatever position he has at the time. In all matters, Uranus expresses the Superior Will.

Though man may make many decisions as the result of his own desires or knowledge, he must also realize that the Superior Will, which he calls God, is aware of conditions far beyond finite thought or mortal knowledge of what is to be. Therefore, this Superconscious Will, directed against man's desire or will, demands that he follow a course which to him is out of line with the plans he may have for his own best interests. This conflict between the superconscious awareness developing under Uranus aspects and what seem practical attitudes creates a restless, uncertain and unsettled state of mind or of soul. The individual is torn between what he thinks is intelligent and in line with reasonable thought, and what is the demand of Divine Will, that the soul be given more experience, however unwilling the self may be to change.

In these periods of uncertainty, there is one rule of utmost importance. The native should do absolutely nothing which is the result of his own thinking when Uranus is in conjunction or adverse aspect to any planet in the natal chart, for what will be done under those conditions will not be what the Divine Will demands. He should wait, and realize that whatever comes to pass is the will of the Highest. When a change comes that is completely without precedent and at variance with his desire, he should think that within a period of nine years or less whatever came to pass under the disruptive aspect of Uranus will prove more important for future growth than any former pattern which might have resulted from one's own choice.

This is because Divine Will knows the distant future as well as the immediate profit of the moment, and has a preview of all future time. Admittedly, this may seem not to take into account an individual's present needs.

When the changes caused by Uranus destroy what exists in the present, what was once unwelcome may prove within a fairly short period to be the greatest possible blessing. What seems calamity coming to pass in this decade can be the beginning of a period of far better thought, far greater spiritual comprehension and more vitally important change than would be made by any man willingly. This new era must come to pass if man is to make progress forward.

23
Neptune Contact with the Spirit

Neptune is the intangible quality of Omnipotence. Man knows God only through what God creates in form and expresses through man's thought; and through man himself, if he accepts literally, as many do, the thought that he is created "in the image of God."

Man lives, therefore, only as long as he has within himself what is called spirit. Spirit, through which God is made manifest, is the vital quality integrated into the human embryo in the period of quickening. Without it, no life comes into being. Thus Neptune may be considered the form of the Creator that is incorporate in each mortal, animal, plant and even mineral form. In plant life this invisible quality of God manifests itself the moment a seed is so saturated with moisture that it can convert Neptune's vapor into liqud; it assists the earth in developing the seed into flower, fruit or grain.

Therefore, it is as necessary as breathing to take into human life the liquid quality of Neptune. But liquids may be of two types. The destructive forms are drugs, alcohol and all stimulants by which man seeks to assist nature in creating something resembling nature's vitality. Like its destructive nature, Neptune's constructive nature is synthetic, but its constructive quality relates to the sea, over which it has rulership. In the water of the ocean are found many forms of mineral substance, plus vegetable life, more conducive to perfection of inner growth than anything man can create.

The average man's concept of Neptune, however, is that it is deceptive and variable, like the sea. One cannot be sure what is the true color of the sea and what is the reflected color of the sky above, since Neptune shows all things through reflecting the light of the Sun. Even the photographed image, Neptune-ruled, is perfected by refracted light rays. The quality of Neptune is infused into sea water through the Sun's orientation to all forms of life in a single liquid—sea water. From the sea, through the vaporizing action that draws clouds of mist skyward, the Sun distills these qualities, to release them later as rain.

The affinity of Neptune matter with solid matter may be seen along any sandy beach, as waves rush forward toward the sand, cover it briefly and are soon absorbed. In this way Neptune substance joins with what is completely opposite in nature to bring that contrasting form to full completion; for, without spirit, life is incomplete. Without Neptune's continued activity, the sand upon the rim of the sea would be dissipated by the wind.

Since Neptune seeks to become one with physical life, man too would be intelligent to accept this alliance, for if life lacks spiritual qualities, it is incomplete. In all things, man goes back to first principles. Indeed he is the symbol of these since the amoeba was the first living organism existing in terrestrial space, and shows through its finite form these first principles. To study the substance of self first in embryo–the nucleus of watery substance surrounded by a shell-like shape–is to see Neptune as the original substance of any kind. But what is contained must have some rim or shell to contain it; hence both center and shell are necessary.

The containing shell for Neptunian spirit is man's physical body, which fends off the intrusions of material contact from the spirit within the soul. Without the barrier of soul (the etheric body) and physical form, spirit would know the most crushing onslaught from contact with earthly experience and much that is a part of the soul's necessary education.

What is the soul's function? It is to integrate the several principles of man. In itself, it is that part of man's fourfold nature that is in the temporary but inescapable bondage of both soul and spirit, so that spirit may not escape from the body until death, but continues to exist therein, though too often in embryo. Spiritual thought is necessary, however, if the spirit is to transcend mere survival. If there is no such thought nor contact through prayer with the Highest Source, the spirit is so ill-nourished that it cannot grow. Like a seed planted in dry soil, it remains dormant. Therefore, prayer is necessary if man is ever to become aware of the Christ within.

Like the embryo of a bird, Neptune substance grows only through what is supplied from within the shell, not by means of the shell itself. The shell is still intact when the first peck from within reveals life fully developed in form. Within each man is the same potential for growth and magnificent development, but it remains only a potential unless growth comes through the spiritual quality of Neptune.

Spirit is intangible. It is love. It is beauty. It shows itself in the growth of the soul in every instance of giving to another the best of the self.

Man becomes good only by being good. He becomes whatever he is because that is what he desires to be, for without desire there is no attainment. But simply expressing desire does not always result in accomplishment.

Neptune rules quality of substance, not quantity. Quality seems less practical and man therefore thinks it less desirable, but it is far more necessary. If man understands life as a part of long integrated epochs through which the growth of the soul continues via the cultivation of Neptune's constructive thought, he may seek to grow toward eternal oneness with all souls, not merely toward greater physical strength or more economic security. Each individual lifetime is only a brief space in eternal time for the soul, imprisoned within the self to better acquaint the spirit with the situations, opportunities, temptations, necessities and adventures of each lifetime.

Though man may feel that his first need is financial security, it is even more necessary to educate, through all kinds of experiences, the inner self, the etheric form wherein the spirit dwells. Therefore, man needs the Neptune quality of constructive thought. It is essential for the growth of the eternal spiritual monad and is offered by the Omnipotent Source to nourish man's stimulating, activating principle. Such stimulation of the soul would not be necessary if man could function without this principle, but if one observes the corpse from which the soul has escaped at death, one sees that it is only insensate matter. Without Neptune's quality, it cannot continue to function or exist. But the escaped soul, mental body and spirit do not die. They continue to exist in higher planes of vibratory force. Therefore, man ought to think more about the cultivation of qualities necessary to the eternal part of himself rather than what is transitory and passes in less than a second of eternal time.

Since the Omnipotent Mind, through which the Creator instructs that which He created, does not teach the self through Neptune's type of thought, man must assist the soul, in its education, through each experience in life. It is only by cultivating all manner of beauty and selfless thought that the eternal soul is given Neptune's substance. This is made available in succeding periods of life if spiritual thought is repeatedly read, spoken, understood and integrated into the personality. Man should not pray because he desires benefit, as he too often does. He should pray to become a part of Omnipotent Truth; for without this contact his soul cannot progress.

Man may think he lives well and succeeds without prayer, if living well is enjoying material pleasures only, but when he leaves the physical body, what survives? A soul which is so poorly supplied with the essentials for growth that it can hardly exist in the eternal verities of the hereafter. The soul has lived many times before the present life, but from each living it must gain some added growth. May one not think, as those of the Orient, that the more the soul grows, the sooner it becomes at one with all other souls? The more of Neptune's spiritual food it receives, the sooner it ascends to the highest level in the evolutionary spiral of growth that leads to the Pinnacle of Truth.

Neptune could be called the educator of the soul, the link between God and all souls that offer good freely to others without thought of compensation. If man cannot serve God at the altar or devise other ways of service, he may express devotion and fair thought in service to his fellow-men and in tender care for the lesser creatures of the earth. So truly do those of one of the great faiths of the Orient understand this that it is the duty of some monks to plant at least one tree, so that nature, which is one expression of God, is better supplied with beauty. Man may serve his concept of good, which he calls God, in many ways. To discover the channel through which each individual gives this service, he should look to the house ruled by Neptune, along with the position of Neptune, in the natal chart.

Like all planets, however, Neptune can show such afflictions in the birth chart that its influence is strange and destructive, rather than constructive. The dreamers, the wishful thinkers, the would-be artists, the pseudo-intellectuals who see no necessity for work of a practical nature —all represent a part of Neptune's destructive quality. Many kinds of awareness must make contact with the Omnipotent Mind through Neptune for the Omnipotent Mind incorporates all truth learned by billions of souls' experiences. Much which might seem worthless still has value, since it reveals to the Omnipotent Mind how a soul sought truth but was misled or deceived. Those who desire to become good but fail to do so come to this condition because they blame others, not themselves, for what they failed to be. This is why Neptune often is blamed by those who seek to escape the realities of life and self through the use of drugs, liquor and other means. Weak men are those who choose to attain spiritual ends by the easiest way, only to find it is the wrong way.

The Neptune-type often is one who sees things which are worthless from the materialistic standpoint as most necessary, for Neptune rules intangible good expressed in art, music, words or action. But good can be debased through man's earthly experience. What began as desire to become good becomes, through unwillingness to serve other than the self, indifference, inefficiency and total incompetence of conduct. Neptune is the master of all planes of illusion and deception, from the illusion created for entertainment to the illusion man knows of fundamental truth.

Many things may exist in Neptunian form that are unrealized until they become apparent through some formal manifestation of the thought associated with Neptune. Such manifestations are not unreal, for unreality is only unfamiliarity. They are not supernâtural, but supernormal, or beyond the present attainment of those regarded as normal. The abnormal is the result of adverse aspects of Neptune in the birth chart.

Those so afflicted by Neptune yield to the demands made on the soul to know certain experiences, even though such situations conflict with the individual's rigid attitude of proper conduct. Therefore, many who appear abnormal in dress and behavior do so because they cannot overcome the superconscious quality of Neptune thought which continuously impinges on them. A man therefore may be either abnormal and unbalanced, or supernormal and aware of more than other men know, if he has contact with the Neptune quality of thought that causes him to differ mentally from those of similar opportunity and background.

Many regarded as completely normal do what animals do—behave like all others of their kind, under the same circumstances. If one dog barks, all join in the chorus of protesting and indignant noises. If one sees that cats can be chased, all join in the chase. This is the herd instinct, to which man also reacts.

If a man's opinion on a given matter opposes the majority's, many see him as abnormal, unintelligent and unacceptable. Only those of greatest courage demand the right to express fully the quality of the soul, regardless of how it conflicts with the opinion of the masses. These are either the leaders or the outcasts of society, since they refuse to conform.

Thus the Neptune-type is hard pressed by social conditions, since he is pressured by society's critical reaction to any conduct different from that of the majority. He yields to the demand of the superconscious, even though this often makes him an outcast, pervert and one out of place in today's world. Such individuals do what is compelled by the quality of personality with which they were born in the present incarnation. They are forced to express this inner demand of Neptune; therefore, it is unreasonable to condemn them and important to understand that they have no will strong enough to discipline Neptune's influence.

Thus conduct resulting from the square, opposition or conjunction of Neptune to important planets produces distorted personalities born into their unhappy situation because in a past life they failed to do what was required to produce proper growth of the soul. For this they are sent back to a bitter hell on earth.

Neptune does not afflict the soul only. It can afflict the self also, since the soul demands expression through physical form. When Neptune afflicts the mind, the individual is impractical or lacking intelligent thought, and must either conform to the ideas of the masses or be conditioned for a place in the world by learning to do what conflicts with his inner will. The result is a distorted type of personality, due to the soul's effort to maintain command over the life.

This planet can produce hallucinations so vivid that those who suffer from Neptune afflictions become abject slaves to all forms of vice. When in adverse aspect to Mercury, it can create illusions so vivid that those who might have put the mind to practical use produce the most fantastic and unrealistic material and thought.

Under the transit of Neptune to Mercury or to any planet, the notion comes to those persons who previously thought in a perfectly normal manner that some unknown mind can and does intrude upon theirs. Thoughts strange and unlike the usual way of thinking come from a

Neptunian source and manifest themselves either as fantasy or even, in some instances, as possession.

In sleep, all men come under Neptune's control through dreams. Unwelcome as many such dreams are, they intrude the moment the conscious mind is dormant and not in full command. Such thoughts, forced into the mind, can integrate themselves as fully into the personality and way of thinking as thought in waking hours.

But Neptune does not deal chiefly in trivia. It creates the most intelligent but revolutionary kind of thought. It controls not only psychic manifestations but all phases of mental activity by integrating the superconscious mind and conscious thought. In dreams, this influence often takes symbolic form, creating images that would have been rejected or censored during periods of consciousness. During sleep, such ideas are free to impress the mind and thus influence the quality of the soul's growth.

According to the evolution of the self, the soul responds in dreams to temptation of fact, form and condition. Neptune is the censor of the soul, but is concerned only with what the soul accepts or permits. Man's conscious mind censors what the self does, and is more likely to reject what might be criticized by the world than what is evil to the soul.

Neptune searches the soul to determine its state of growth, and, if man recalls dreams and his response to them, he may discover the condition of his soul from the standpoint of ethical growth. If, in the dream state, he does something so shabby, so insincere, so selfish that he would hesitate to repeat that action in a public place, his soul is showing, according to Neptune something which the individual would not wish to admit openly.

Neptune may be considered, therefore, as overlord of the whole personality, since the self is only the shell, conditioned by the soul's quality of thought and the spirit's activating force. It is strange, therefore, that man is so concerned with getting practical knowledge, gaining social status and making financial progress instead of appraising the quality and progress achieved by his soul. The only reason he came into incarnation was to continue the soul's education. Yet man spends far more time training and educating his mind for some fifty years of productive life on earth that he spends on preparing the soul for the eternal verities.

The destructive quality of Neptune develops because man is so indifferent to quality of thought that his spirit is contaminated, and Neptune is manifested in its lowest forms. In man's present state, he seems completely disintegrated spiritually. He sees more necessities than ever before from the material standpoint, but seldom the daily necessity for prostration of the self before the Omnipotent Whole. Thus the modern and materialistic age shows a quality of afflicted Neptune thought far removed from the purpose for which Neptune is a part of all life.

Though man is one infinitesimal part of Highest Thought, he is so poorly aware, through any comprehension of present theological teachings, that he considers good to be only a willingness to attend services held periodically in some house of worship. It is not his thought that the soul may be cultivated and grow through thinking well of all his fellowmen or through offering a quality of love that desires only the best conditions for others. Thus he expresses only a small part of Neptune's finest attributes.

Neptune, symbolized by the shaft of illumination from the Source impenetrating the cup of the Moon of man's soul, is spirit which, integrated into man's conscious mind, awakens his soul and in time can show full expression through the attitudes and actions of the self. It inspires him to desire a high quality of thought in each incarnation and to express such quality of progress in constructive attitudes.

Until many men feel this desire, mankind must wait in vain to create a better world and gain a new awareness of truth.

24
Pluto
The Destroyer

Pluto, like all planets, originated from the Omnipotent Whole. Therefore, even in this–the most remote of the so-called malefics–there must be something of the nature of the Creator of all solar systems. But Pluto and Scorpio, the sign it rules, so completely integrate the concept of Lucifer, the fallen angel, that Pluto might be considered of dual nature. Lucifer, in allegory, fell from the Highest Source to Hell because he defied God's laws. Pluto, like Lucifer, rebels against good or constructive growth. This opposition is made manifest in the nature of the force it exerts against the cohesive and consolidating effect of the central source, the Sun.

Yet within the Source are all qualities incorporated; whatever is a part of the Omnipotent Whole must partake of the nature of good as well as of evil.

Evil is form, as opposed to spirit or non-form. Form is self. The integration of spirit into self at mortal birth gives man the awareness of One within, the realization each individual comes to have that in some measure he is an infinitesimal part of the Omnipotent Whole. Therefore, while man appears to be Lucifer in form, within is spirit; and when each man parts from mortal life, spirit does not die. Only the body is destroyed. Spirit escapes and returns to the spirit world, eternal and all-enduring.

Form necessarily descends—falls, as did Lucifer—from the Highest Source, through sexual service required of man to create life, since only through sexual functioning is physical life created. Therefore, although sexual power might be thought of as God's most magnificent gift to man, man has degraded that gift into the basest form of self-abuse by using it for the gratification of the self, not solely for the purpose of procreation, for which it was given him.

Pluto, symbol of the sexual, creative capacity, personifies the descent of form from spiritual quality. Body and spirit are continuously at war; hence Lucifer is frequently portrayed as defying God, for he represents each mortal's body which is in rebellion against what spirit directs. Only by accepting such direction, however, can man come to the degree of awareness in which he realizes this conflict or manifest spiritual strength to the degree that others become aware of it.

Spirit integrated into the body produces mortal beginnings. In that instant when it departs from the body, the process of disintegration and decay of the body begins. Therefore, Pluto, the destroyer, fills one of the most vital functions in mortal life, both as the means of finite creation and as the power through which spirit is released from the body at the termination of each mortal incarnation.

The trinity is known in the Christian faith as the

Creator or Father, the Christ or Son, and the Holy Ghost. Without this trinity there can be no complete functioning. God, the Creator, is Divine Will, intending, devising and demanding that spirit enter into the process resulting eventually in finite form. Following the will to create comes knowledge as awareness of the need to create. These are the qualities of God expressed through highest intelligence, born of the Father; hence the Christ-consciousness. In oriental thought two corresponding persons who comprise a trinity are Brahma and Krishna. The third is Shiva, the destroyer of life.

Shiva and Pluto are of the same nature, for is it not true that from the moment sex creates life a process of destruction begins? Constructive growth can only continue until full maturity is reached, after which Pluto begins the destruction of old or outmoded form and in time permits the release of spirit through what man calls death. Pluto is, in Christian faith, completely concealed under what, because of association with the Christ principle, is accepted as Divine Thought. What would mortals think were they told that destruction of physical life is the thought of the Omnipotent Will when that life ceases to grow constructively and has begun the process of disintegration? Man is so convinced of the great importance of the physical self that he cannot conceive of One who, in Omnipotent Wisdom, knows that until spirit is released from the body, progress of the soul is limited to what the failing self permits.

Pluto, as ruler of the sign ruling the sexual organs, is considerably more appreciated, since the ability to create life is regarded as God's blessed gift. Few indeed think of another value of Pluto-ruled power: the transmutation of creative energy into a state in which it stimulates the occult sensitivity and broadens the capacity of the mind to grow far beyond what is ordinary. Why otherwise do members of the Catholic priesthood and many of the greatest minds of oriental lands find celibacy essential? Certainly it is not because men of such caliber would produce ill-begotten children. It is because they realize that in the repeated or continued use of this power to produce life, in the stupid waste of the vital essence for self-gratification, or in the idea that such usage creates more spiritual and lasting marital bonds, this energy potential is wasted and eventually destroyed.

Neither can man realize that the misuse of Pluto's creative power increases destructive processes, in that the universe is reacting to the nature of its component parts. If everywhere there is destruction of physical life and of the higher potentials incorporate in life, all activity in the present day must be much more destructive than constructive. Through complete cooperation with Pluto's destructive nature, man is speeding up in every possible way the destruction of finite matter. In misuse of sexual power, in continued war, in waste of earth's natural God-given resources, in more and more indifference to constructive and creative conditioning, he is assisting Pluto to destroy life. But what results from this continued destructive process? Tremendous energy is created, to be returned to the Source. What would seem loss to finite minds is, to the cosmos, only the necessary transformation of matter into energy. From material things which have fallen into decay, new form or spiritual force comes into being through various methods of conversion of matter to higher form.

This transformation, initiated by Pluto, is the everlasting, eternal and essential destruction of matter, which results in the creation of energy. A simple example may be seen in the burning of a log. The log of wood is matter. Direct flame to it in the fireplace, and, in a few moments, it will be ignited and will give forth heat—a result of the destruction of matter. The log is destroyed, but there is something more than ashes which proves that it existed. What Pluto released was heat, or a form of energy which, like spirit, is within matter.

This process of creation and destruction of form or the creation of matter and then its destruction to create cosmic energy is continuous, as is the process of life, growth, dissolution and death. From the central power source, the Sun, matter is formed and expelled into planetary orbits. Like mortal life, it increases in time to fullest potential; then, as planetary orbits fall away from the center, form decreases until, as Pluto, the outermost planet of our universe, illustrates, final form is attained and what has been destroyed returns to cosmic space as energy to recharge the solar system.

Transits of Pluto or aspects from it in the personal chart always destroy some outworn condition in the life, clearing the way for development on a higher level. Adverse aspects destroy, but fortunate transits combine with other favorable planetary transits to create better conditions.

With Pluto's entrance into Leo in mid-1938 sexual relationships resulting from physical expression of the emotions, hitherto repressed by discipline or convention, began to come into such prominence that most of the civilized world found itself faced with a new problem: sexual relations among those so young that their actions constituted a real sexual revolution. Pluto in Leo started the destruction of all old kinds of creative activity connected with the natural fifth house sign (hence children) as well as creative ideas. Education discarded old modes of expression and cleared the way for another type of development. From 1938 until 1956 this process of destruction continued, but the immediate result was not to bring better conditions in relation to fifth house matters, but fantastic and deceptive ones, for as Pluto left Leo, Neptune entered the Pluto-ruled sign Scorpio, giving those long indifferent to the old ideals of creativity or sexuality such unrealistic attitudes that sex became an obsession. Music, art, the theater and, most of all, the Neptune-ruled motion pictures glorified sex and placed it in a completely unreal role in all levels of life. Until the planet of illusion lets man see clearly the results of sex for self-gratification rather than procreation, the world will not recover from Pluto's destruction. The most revealing insight into this attitude was shown in the widespread opposition to the Catholic church's pronouncements against birth control.

Neither widespread venereal disease, many deaths from abortion nor population explosions in countries in which uncontrolled sex created more children than could be fed sufficed to convince man that sex could destroy as well as create life. Pluto's destructive process becomes obvious only to those who look, as the astrologer should, at the slow movement of the destroyer passing through each sign to bring to termination whatever that sign rules.

Those who are philosophers as well as astrologers, however, may see, in what seems a long period of self-destruction, the necessary prelude to a future time when conditions now accepted as completely rational and satisfactory will culminate in Pluto's destruction of all which ceases to show constructive growth. Such termination promises future generations a finer world, a better life and more progress on the evolutionary spiral toward the Highest Source than could have been possible without Pluto's destruction.

Because the discovery of Pluto was recent compared to those of other planets, and its transit slow, students find less adequate information regarding the transits of this distant planet through the signs than is available for other planets. Therefore, a summary of the nature of events resulting from Pluto's past transits and an estimate of future effects may be helpful.

While Pluto definitely influences individuals, and the effects of its aspects by transit are readily seen, particularly in the charts of those with many planets in Scorpio, the sign it rules, the effect of Pluto on world conditions as it passed through the signs from Capricorn through Libra was also very apparent.

In both the individual chart and the chart of a nation or of the world, Pluto terminates any condition which has ceased to show constructive growth and clears the way for some future planetary aspect to create a new and better form of whatever the transited house or sign rules.

On account of the variation in time periods which Pluto shows in transiting the various signs, the mundane-sign transits of this planet are sometimes as short as twelve years to a sign, sometimes as long as thirty-two; but within those transits many terminations of old forms concerned with the particular sign take place.

Capricorn, natural ruler of the tenth house of government, knew Pluto's transit in the years from 1762 to 1777. Americans remember this as the period when the divine right of George III to rule the American colonies in the western world was challenged and overthrown, and a democratic form of government was established.

In 1777, Pluto came into the sign Aquarius, remaining there until 1799. This was the time when the demand for "liberty, equality and fraternity" was heard in France, terminating with a revolution in which another royal ruler lost his throne and a new form of government, giving greater rights to the common man, came into being.

Since Pisces, a water sign, rules matters connected with the sea, the effect of Pluto's transit in this sign from 1799 to 1823 terminated the old form of ocean transportation by sailing vessels and cleared the way for better forms of navigation. Pisces also rules asylums and prisons; Pluto's transit brought to an end some of the terrible institutional conditions which degraded, brutalized and gave no care of any kind to the criminal and the insane.

Pluto's transit of Aries from 1823 to 1852 was the

period of exploration of new territory in America, settlement by whites of formerly virgin lands, wars against Indian tribes, and the birth of a new kind of world in America with conquest as the keynote of progress. From the intellectual or spiritual standpoint, Pluto in the Mars-ruled sign brought little progress; man was too interested in self-expression through subjugation of other men and domination of minority groups by conquest. This is logical; a planet of Pluto's destructive nature was passing through the sign which constructively gives birth to new frontiers but destructively terminates old forms and former ways of life.

In 1852 Pluto entered the materialistic sign Taurus, remaining there until 1884. This was a period when old ways of gaining possessions and making income were phased out, and farm and shop labor was performed by machinery. The transit of Pluto wiped out slave labor in the south, destroying the economy of much of America. In the north, low-paid workers organized to demand a larger share of their products, and in order to increase production, machines came into use to replace manual labor. The world picture was changed by the destruction of slow and costly ways of production and the stepping up of profits.

Many still living remember the changes which took place from 1884 to 1914 with Pluto in the Mercury-ruled sign Gemini, which governs transportation, communication and local publications. The telephone became a household and business necessity; the motorcar took the place of the old horse and buggy or horse-drawn delivery wagon; and roads adequate for old forms of travel were paved and extended for thousands of miles to bring neighboring communities in closer contact with one another. Postal service was speeded up by the introduction of air mail, and the use of train transportation for short journeys started to decline; with good roads and more privately owned motor cars, families traveled by automobile and lighter freight was shipped by truck. Pluto in Mercury's sign thus destroyed the former modes of travel and communication, and by the start of World War I, the Gemini-ruled American people had entered a new way of life.

When Pluto entered Moon-ruled Cancer in 1914, most of Europe was at war, and with America's continued involvement, manpower so declined that women for the first time found a place in industry, the office and in many types of work formerly open to men only. The result was a complete destruction of the old ways of life in the home. New labor-saving devices were produced to take the place of the work women formerly did. Paternal authority seemed to decline with woman's added economic importance, and male dominance in the family suffered because of such competition. By 1939, when postwar prosperity and freedom had worked drastic changes in the family picture, the home in America, as well as in other parts of the world, was so changed–economically, and in relation to the position of women–that Pluto's effect while in Leo was a natural result.

An emphasis on the child's right to express freely his own personality resulted in a generation of rebels without a cause (other than resentment against the results of war in

Europe). America rode high in postdepression prosperity; children were indulged in every way; old forms of primary education were considered unsuitable for the youth of the day, and schools underwent radical changes. The theater was no longer the favorite form of public entertainment; interest shifted to motion pictures of such elaborate nature that the stage could not compete with them. The first public demonstrations of television came in this period, and television, like the telephone, came to be regarded as essential to every home. Moral attitudes were destroyed by the war, and old forms of creative art became completely unacceptable to the younger generation by 1957.

Pluto in Leo brought many terminations of material circumstances, since Leo is one of the fixed signs. Pluto in the mutable sign Virgo from 1957 to 1972 changed all ideas and methods in connection with matters ruled by the natural sixth house. Old tenements were demolished to make room for federal or state subsidized public housing; many new methods of food preparation were developed, labor groups and those never regarded as part of the labor market struck repeatedly for wage increases. Services once considered essential were replaced by machines; health insurance became a major government project in both the United States and other nations; and the whole idea of *service* was changed.

Pluto entered Libra in 1972 and will remain there until 1984; but, consistent with the destructive effect Pluto causes in other signs, this may be remembered as a period when legal marriage, already threatened by many divorces and many free associations without legal bonds, may either completely change form or find itself one of those old institutions inadequate for the conditions of the time. Business partnerships will come under the same terminal aspect. Something of the impending collapse is to be previewed in the way Uranus created sudden changes as it pretransited through the seventh house sign.

Pluto in the natural eighth house sign Scorpio (1984 to 1995) must be expected to bring changes in relation to all matters of inheritance, changes in disposition of the physical body after death, radical ideas concerning the division of all partnership incomes, and destruction of old ideas in connection with the sexual relationship, already foreshadowed in the increased number of laws regarding formerly abnormal relationships and contraceptive practices. Previous to Pluto's transit of this sign, Neptune in Scorpio will have produced such false standards and idealistic or unreal sexual attitudes that they will only be improved by Pluto's destructive action in the years approaching the close of the present century.

The much-needed destruction of outmoded laws and legal procedure can be anticipated when Pluto transits Sagittarius in the years between 1995 and 2010 as well as the termination of old creeds and present concepts of Divinity. Many ideas and faiths which now seem unlikely to be changed or abandoned will, under Pluto's transit, come to an end, to clear the way for concepts on a higher level of intelligence. Outdated laws will no longer work injustice, and the present pattern of international relationships will, in time, cease to create crises between governments.

When Pluto last transited Capricorn, from 1762 to 1777, rebellion against the divine right of kings brought into being the first democracy in the western continent. Pluto's return in the early part of the twenty-first century (2010 to 2025) to the sign which rules government ought again to repeat the pattern of "off with the old, on with the new," whatever form the new may take.

Aquarius, through which Pluto moves from 2025 to 2047, was in the sign of brotherhood during the period when "liberty, equality and fraternity" came to be heard in France. Then men of lowly birth, but alike in national loyalties and race, demanded the right of self-government and recognition. While it seems unlikely that this demand for equality, augmented to include race and creed, could be so late in reaching a final stage, the transit of Pluto through Aquarius will truly destroy racism throughout the civilized world to create a real "brotherhood of man."

Epilogue

Almost eighteen years have passed since the first chapter of this book was put into oral form on the large tape recorder carried twice monthly to the home of Mrs. Bernice Cabral in Brookline, Massachusetts. There some twenty professional and student astrologers gathered to listen to words which came *through* me, but which definitely did not reflect my own thoughts!

For many years I had received such material, but never, until that time in Brookline, in my area of chief interest, astrology. Each time I received the exact words mentally, only putting them into vocal form for the benefit of those who listened. If the mental "dictation" (as I came to call it) was interrupted at a critical word, I would have no idea what the next word should be but would have to wait for it to impinge upon my mind.

The dictations began in 1941. In 1950 I began to receive material on how one becomes an initiate and eventually a Master; this material eventually filled nine large volumes. It was not until 1958-59, when the Brookline material was dictated to a free class in astrology over a period of two winters, that the dictations concerned astrology. This material, like most of that I had received before, was dictated by a Master who identified himself as Le Compte P. M. St. Germain.

My ability to receive all this material, though a form of mediumship, did not involve any degree of trance or lack of full awareness of everything going on around me. The process of transmission was much the same as that through which the Patience Worth dictations were given to the woman who put many books of them into final form; it was similar to the process described by Ruth Montgomery in her bestseller, *In Search of Truth,* in which she relates how her own mediumship developed.

In my case, though, there was little personal thought offered and much of a religious and philosophical nature, matters in which I had at that time almost no interest. As a newspaperwoman, however, interested in the unusual way in which the information was offered, I recorded most of it.

In their original form, the dictations were marked by the intrusion of two annoying phrases, "Think this" or "Take this thought," and consisted of sentences longer than any which most newspaper editors would have allowed. I made few changes because I thought that no one else would be much interested in reading them. I put the Brookline dictations into manuscript form only when I was told by several professional astrologers that they represented more advanced thought than most books offered. In so doing I have deleted the annoying phrases, made occasional changes to clarify the material and have furnished examples of what the unseen teacher taught.

Therefore, in some parts of this book chapters or parts of them are my own, and are quite different in style from those which were dictated. The reader is often able to differentiate between what is so like a lecturer bent upon expounding astrological concepts and what is my own very informal way of writing.

How is God's plan revealed?

"Astrology is one way in which God—that is, Divine Wisdom—could reveal to man His purpose and plan for each individual. In other words, at the birth of each soul into new incarnation, that soul is offered a pattern which is as true as Truth itself; but those who interpret that pattern are not always able to perceive Truth. Therefore, far more often than not, astrology is so misused, so misinterpreted and so definitely negated in thought that a man uses it to benefit himself; so used, it is of more danger than help. In the conjunction of Uranus, the planet that rules the subject, to Pluto, the destroyer, we saw astrology's old form destroyed: astrology as fortunetelling. Now we see the beginning of a new thought, and know that for the future astrology will be a philosophical and psychological analysis of the self based on the birth chart."

What is the evidence for reincarnation?

"Life is, it continues, it denies death and in a sense sees the eternal verity of a growing soul from life to life. Astrology is, in a way, proof of this. If a man goes through life gaining only the few experiences possible in a single life, there are so many things or experiences he will still lack that he will need to return many times if he is to attain even an iota of the great knowledge to be gained through experience. Astrology points out the capabilities and limitations of each individual; so if one returns many times, each time he gains a new birth chart, a new pattern, a new opportunity. Astrology encourages rebirth, continued soul-growth."

How do we know what we are put here to accomplish in life?

"The position of Saturn in our natal chart points out where our duty lies, for Saturn is the disciplinarian, the great teacher, the source of strength, if strength is what we require. We should perform that duty just as if we were soldiers in the service. This is why so many dread the thought that a Saturn aspect affects the life, since they dread responsibility and do not wish to accept the added burden Saturn places upon them. In the same way the position of Jupiter, the greater benefic, shows the course from which we attain with the least effort, and therefore gain the greatest glory and benefit. Jupiter is the reward for what was done in past lives; the benefic would otherwise not have been given in this life. The chart therefore shows both the place of our duty and service and the source of our benefit. If we serve well in this life, we earn what is a future reward; thus those who accept Saturn's discipline—even though they find it is difficult and demands far greater effort than would otherwise be necessary—deserve, in a sense, the reward gained from doing their duty in a past life.
and demands far greater effort than would otherwise be necessary—deserve, in a sense, the reward gained from

doing their duty in a past life. Just like Saturn and Jupiter, each of the planets shows a definite line of pursuit through Each of the other planets, like Saturn and Jupiter, also shows a definite line of pursuit through which the individual gains.

The personal chart is therefore a complete map that gives you whatever is necessary to know about your equipment, your abilities, your attitudes and, in a sense, your opportunities. Therefore, it is well to follow it in the beginning of your life to the very best of your ability and in the most constructive way possible, if you would gain through the present life the greatest opportunities for the next incarnation."

What determines the need for reincarnation?

"The need for reincarnation is decided by the akashic record, since we who are Masters see every thought and deed, and know every word that the soul knew or had seen fit to speak. We know exactly how evolved the soul is, and whether that soul deserves the opportunity of special service by being permitted to reincarnate, or whether it is necessary to remain for a further period in the astral purgatory so the soul may be purged of errors still in effect. It is far more pleasant to return to earth life than to continue in the astral, because astral life can be a form of real torment, just as dreams, sometimes seen as nightmares, are so dreaded that a man awakes with great relief."

Why must the soul go to the astral plane after death?

"The whole purpose of the astral plane is the purging of the soul, and the soul can only be purged if it goes back in thought for many periods of time and covers all the incidents of the past life. We think it an excellent idea, at the end of each day, for mortals to recall what they have done or failed to do, and if they regret what has been done or said, to put this right as soon as possible, in order not to accumulate a great amount of error to carry into the astral world. Those who do so will know, at the end of their life, little of the self-recrimination of those placed on the astral plane, at the mercy of their own thoughts, for a long period of time."

What and how do the Masters teach?

"We preach what is true, not what is of any creed. We teach Truth through integrating it into the mind—that is, the superconscious mind of any individual capable of receiving our thought. This ability does not depend upon religious or even ethical quality, since it is a quality of the physical-mental complex, capable of tuning in to the vibratory force we exert and by which we transmit the thought-quality offered. This is not illumination, so-called, on the part of the one who receives this thought, and it is not necessarily a religious or spiritual experience. It is simply the attainment of Truth, given in the same way that this thought comes through now—the simple transfer of our thought to another's mind."

(Had I any notion that the dictations I received in past years were due to my spiritual growth, the reference to "physical-mental complex" quickly disabused me of it.)

Is one born to carry out a specific type of work on earth?

"Certainly this is true. There is nothing that is not

part of the Great Plan in which each small, infinitesimal entity plays a part. There are those today who seem to be rebels without causes, decreeing that the present stage of evolutionary progress is decadent and worthless. They are determined to revolt, to destroy completely the deteriorating processes that constitute the modern world. Your hippies are our insurrectionists who propagate the thought that we, the Masters, put to them: through violence, through every form of affront to civilization, false concepts now prevailing will crumble; through this disintegration, a completely new idea, a far greater truth of far more value to the human race will emerge."

(The destructive process seems to have been stepped up in the recent period when Neptune, planet of spirit, passed through Scorpio, the sign ruled by Pluto, the destroyer of outmoded form. While much that resulted from this major transit seems deplorable, it may be the necessary prelude to the destruction of some of the many false standards and hypocritical ideas which have been fostered for many centuries to benefit man's material pursuits—to the detriment of his soul's growth.)

What happens to the mind after it attains the highest plane of ethical awareness?

"The mind is, in a sense, dissolved or impersonalized by the time it enters into oneness with the all-creative force, the exalted period of evolutionary growth. The mind is impersonal compared with the astral soul, which, because it is highly personalized, acts through emotional motives, not merely mental ones. By the time the mind progresses through the plane of Divine or Life Spirit and on to the higher spiritual planes, the self, completely dissipated or absorbed in what is Divine Essence, has ceased to have separate existence. Therefore, we who are Masters do not operate from this exalted plane, because making contact with mortal minds necessitates the assertion of personal qualities of thought that cannot be found on the highest mental plane. There, only Omnipotent Thought exists–the merging of all thought of the highest ethical quality of growth."

Since I am now past eighty and cannot remain on this plane for many more years, I look forward to proving or disproving what passes for truth, not trying to produce harmony while seated on a distant cloud twanging a harp–or busily prodding coals with a pitchfork. Given the choice, I hope that because of past experience I may be assigned to reportorial work, relaying what really exists in the unseen planes to those still earthbound and unconvinced.

Charlotte Harbor, Florida
January, 1976

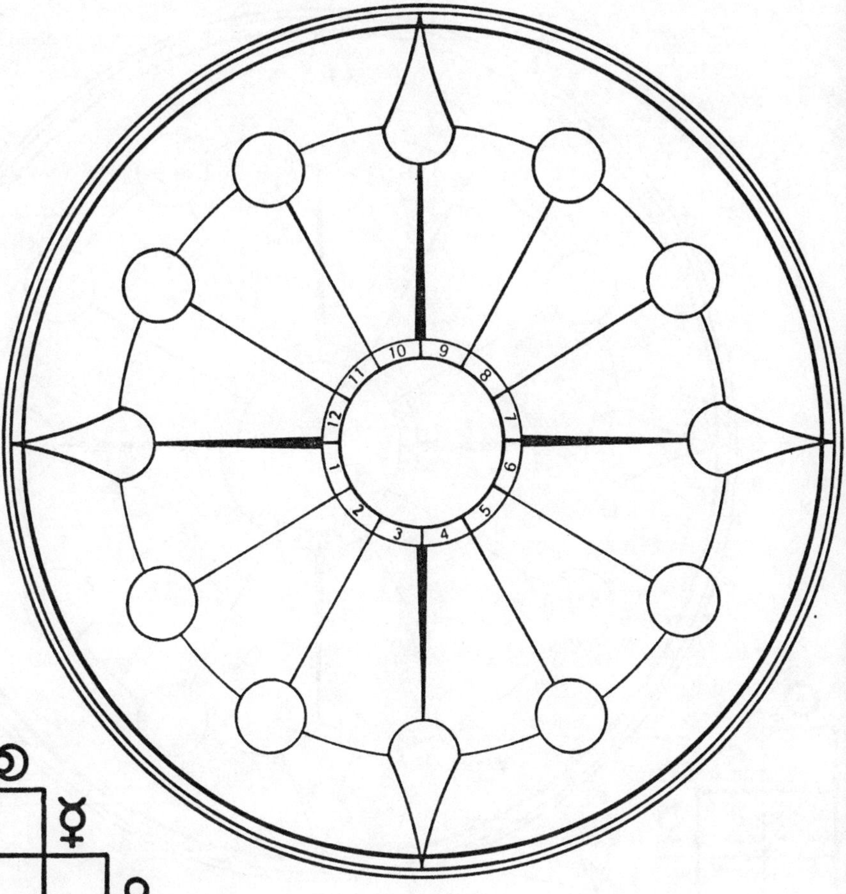

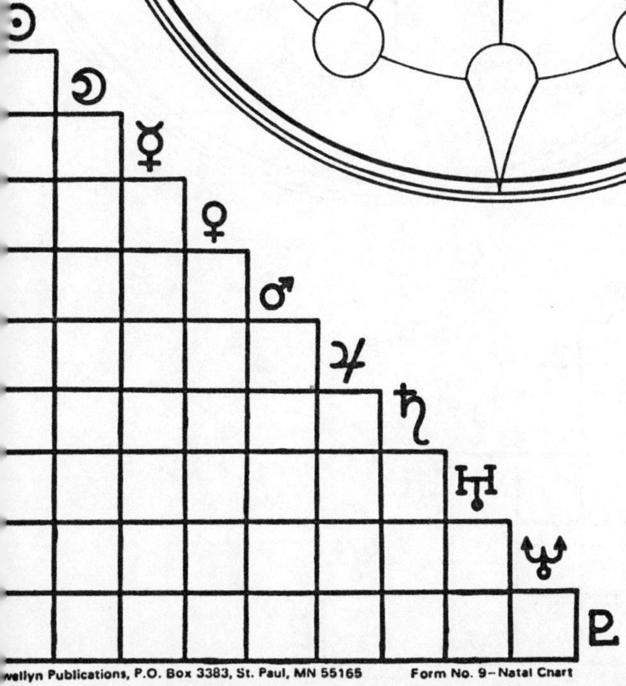

wellyn Publications, P.O. Box 3383, St. Paul, MN 55165 Form No. 9—Natal Chart

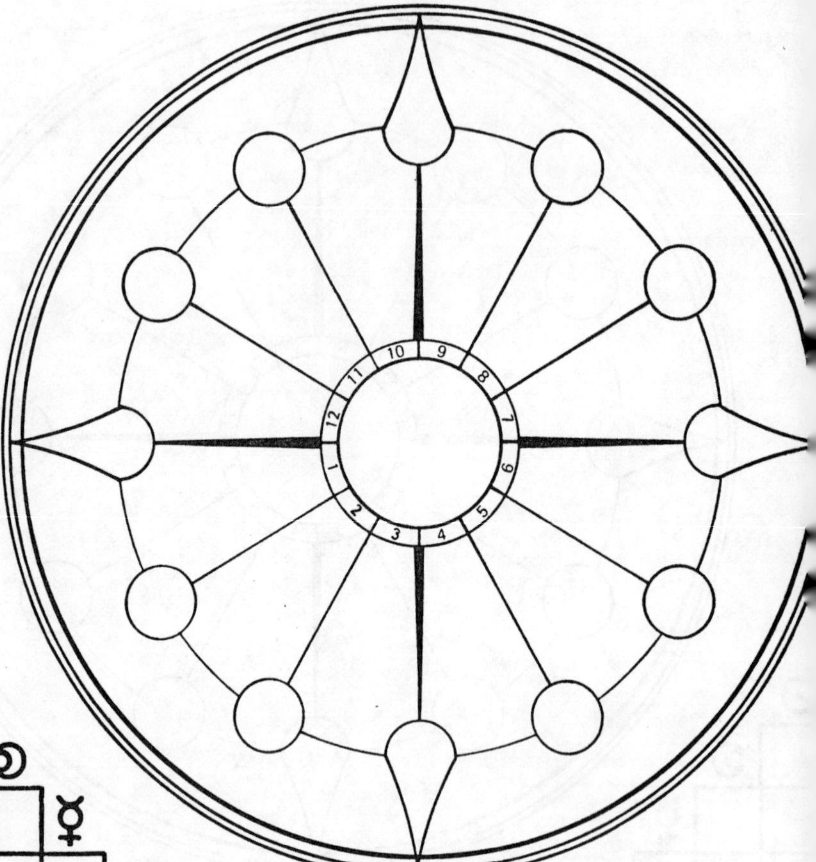

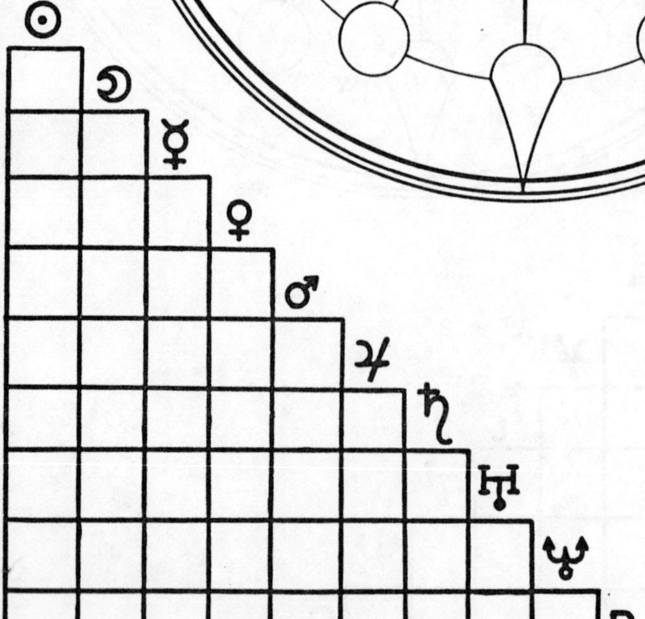

Llewellyn Publications, P.O. Box 3383, St. Paul, MN 55165 Form No. 9—Natal Chart

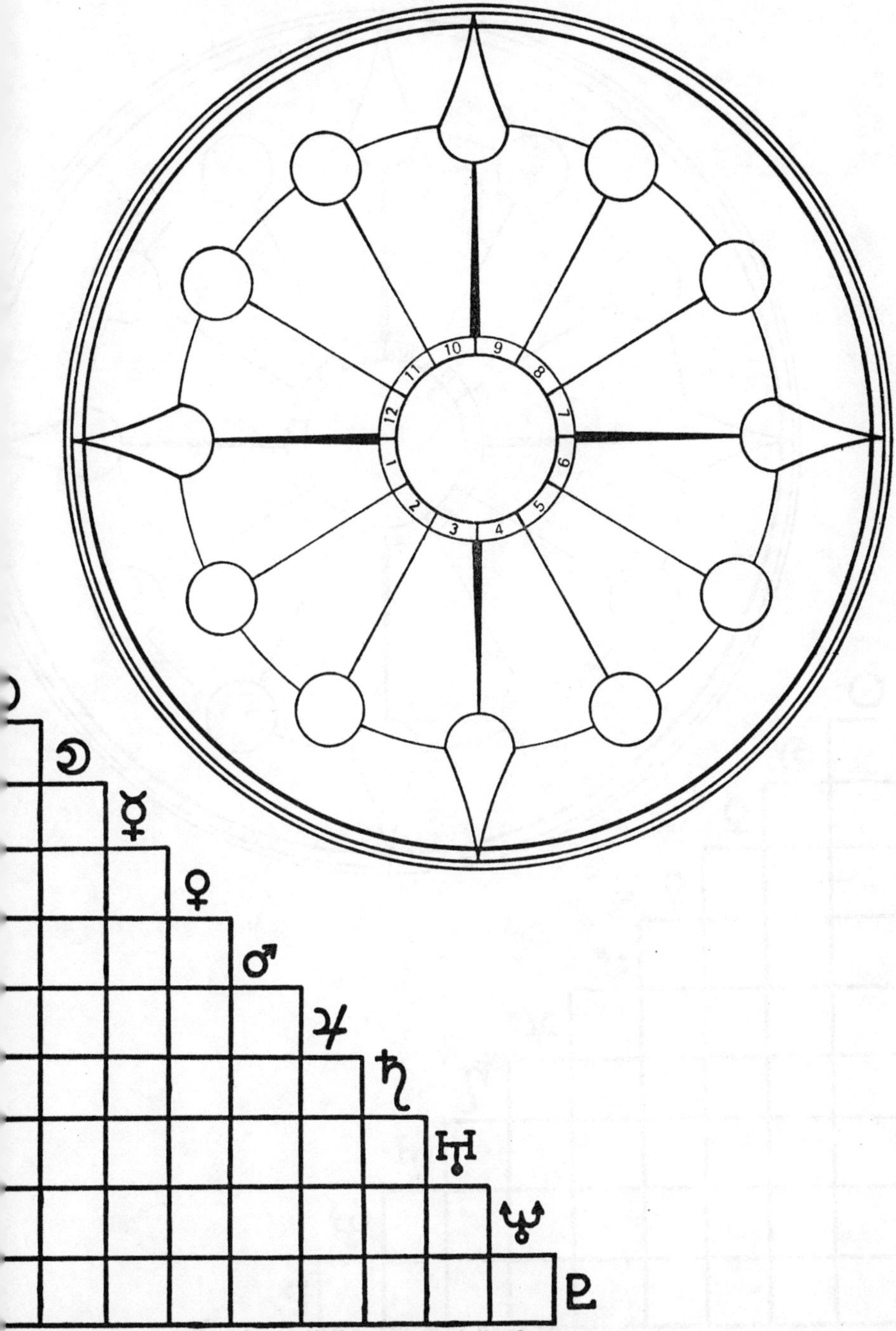
10
9
8
7
6
5
4
3
2
1
12
11

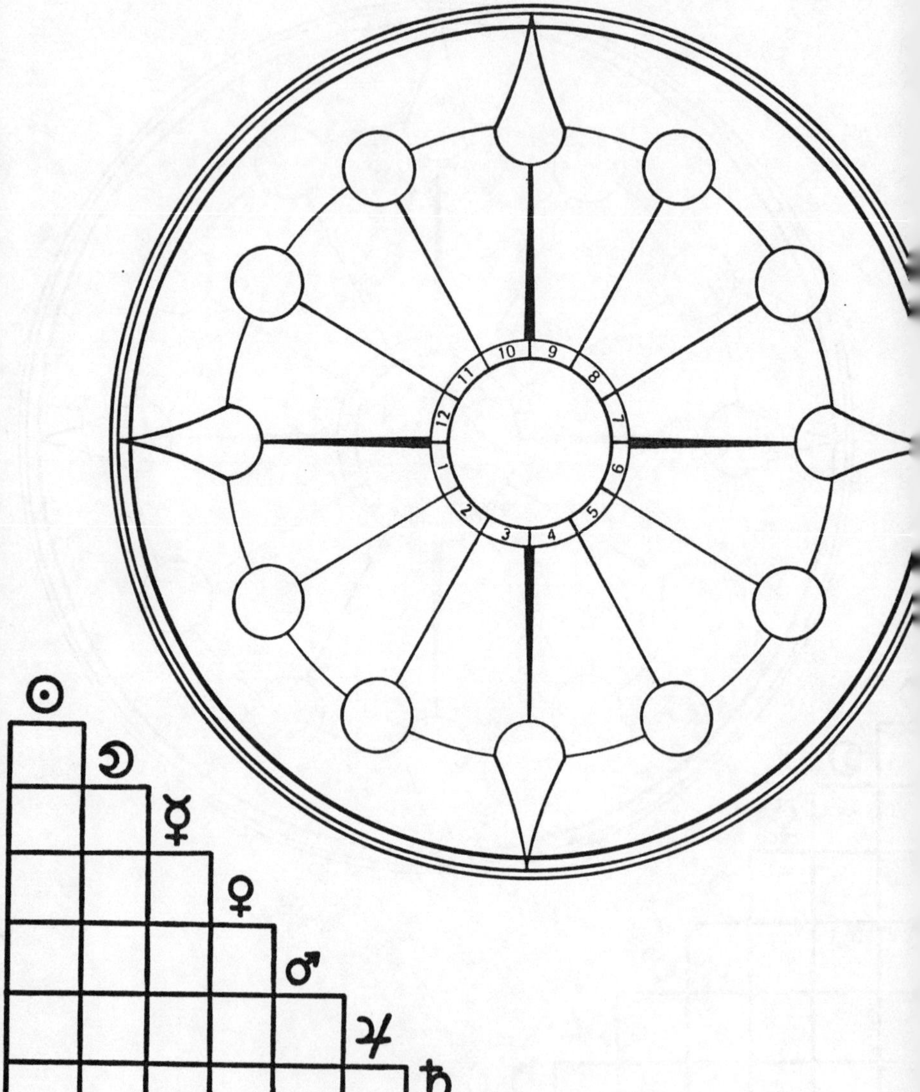

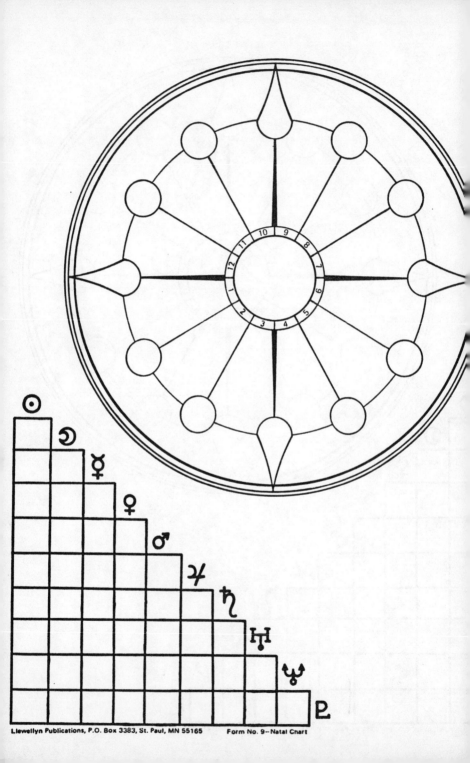

Llewellyn Publications, P.O. Box 3383, St. Paul, MN 55165 Form No. 9—Natal Chart

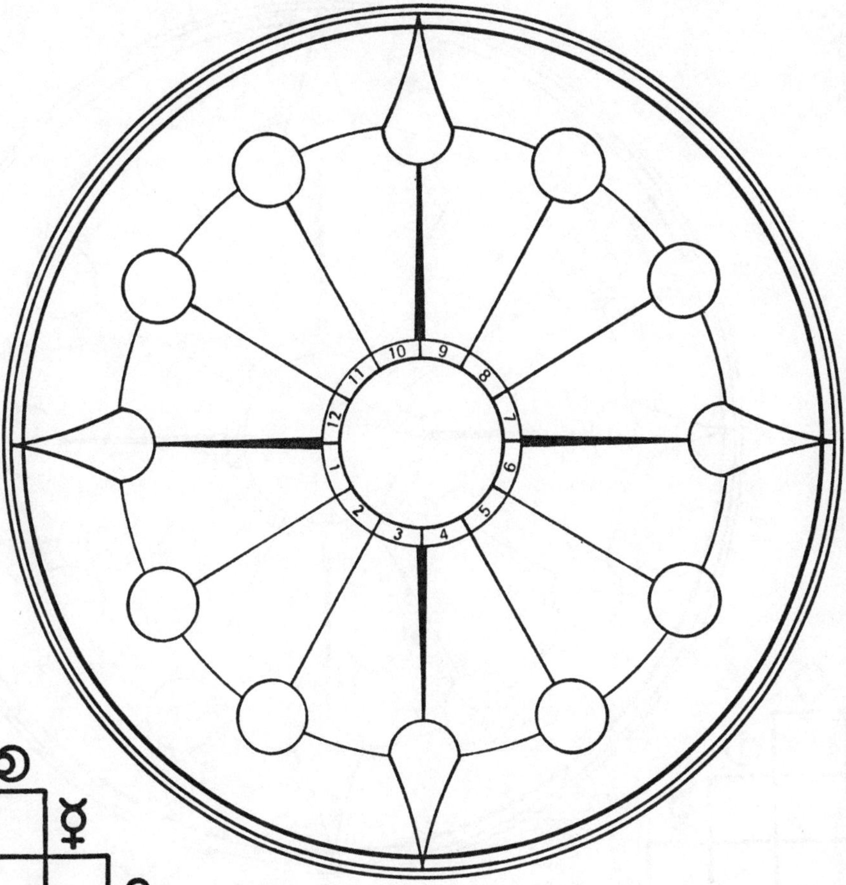

10
9
8
7
6
5
4
3
2
1
12
11

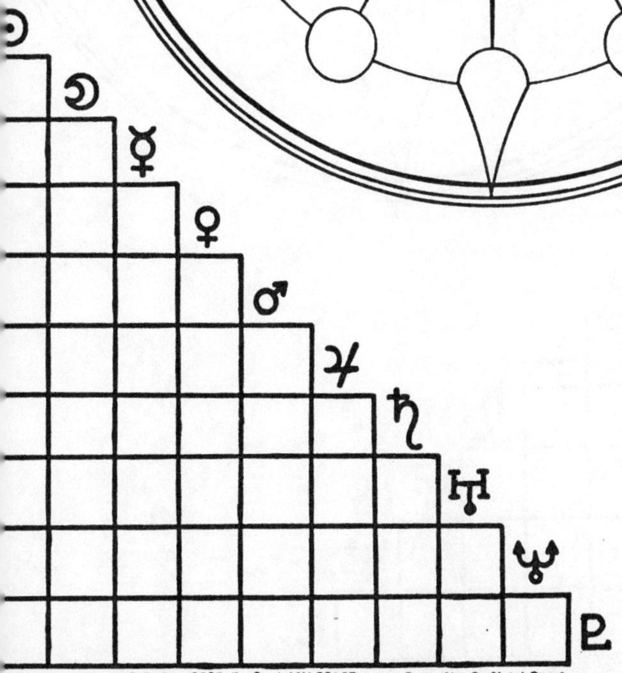

☉
☽
☿
♀
♂
♃
♄
♅
♆
♇

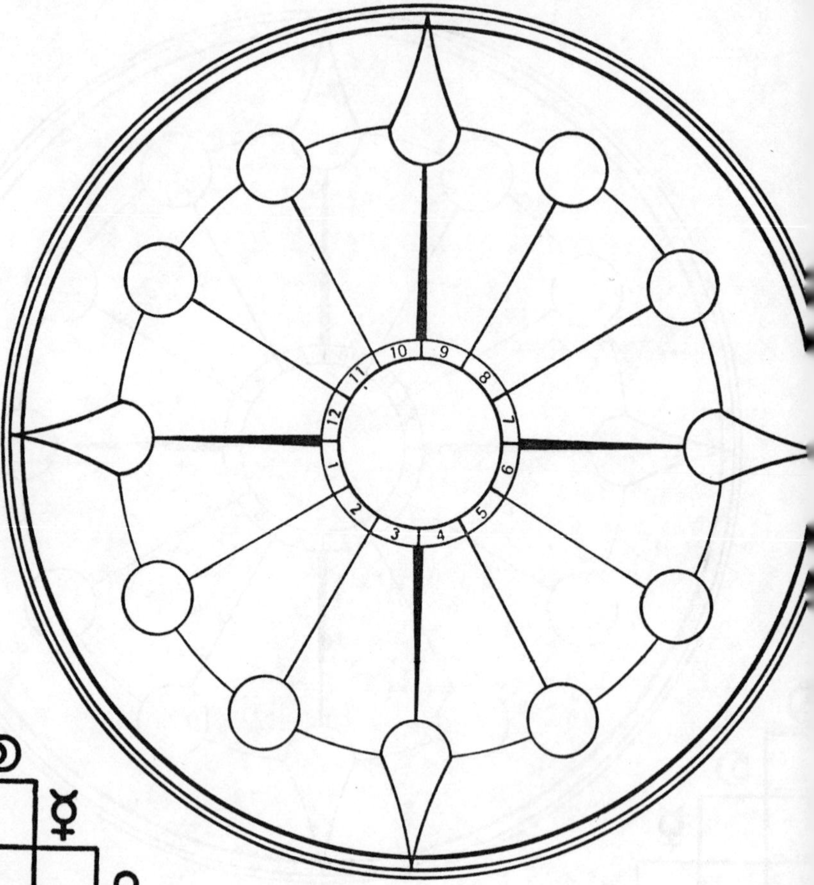

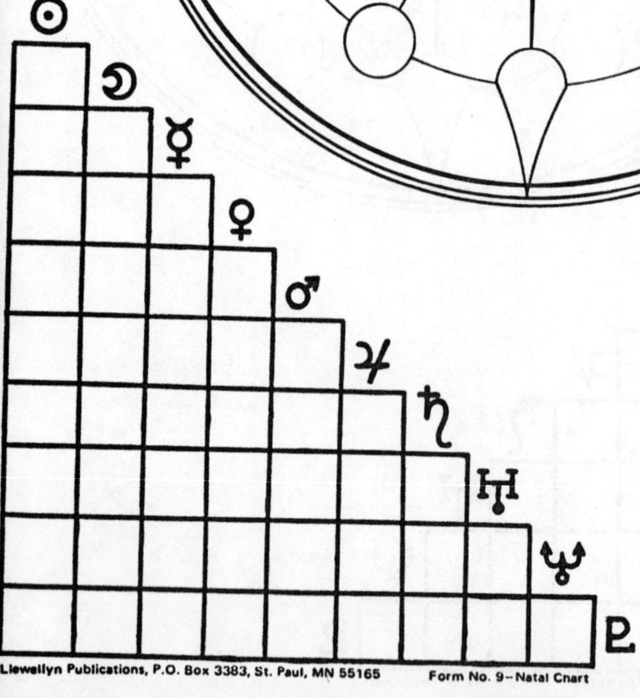

Llewellyn Publications, P.O. Box 3383, St. Paul, MN 55165 Form No. 9—Natal Cnart

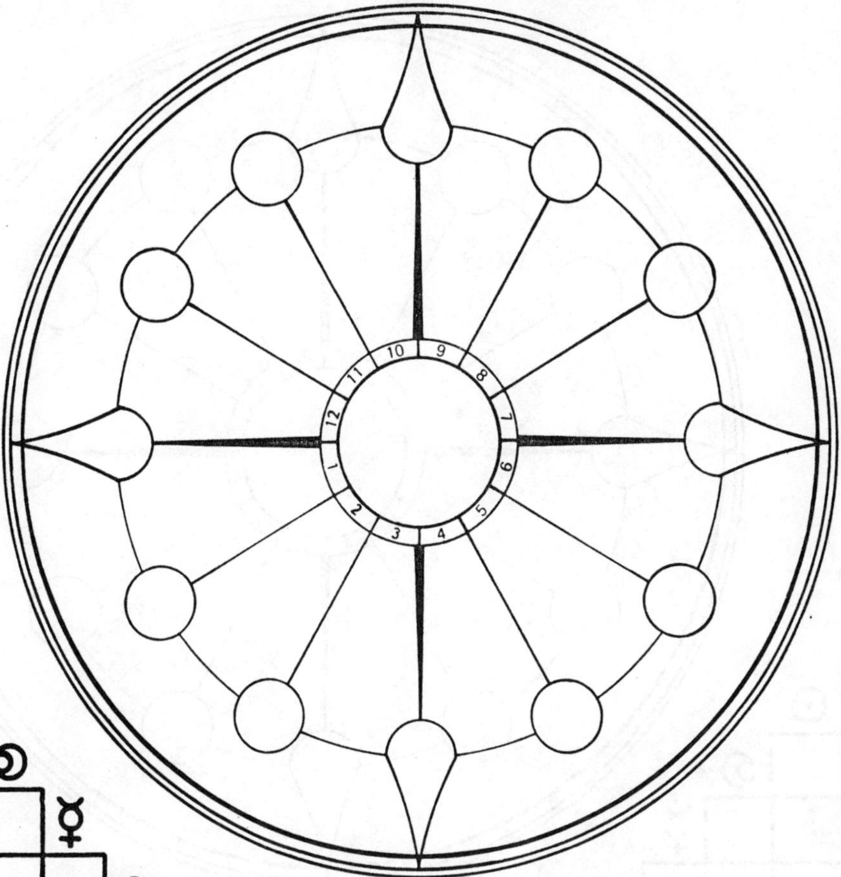
10
9
8
7
6
5
4
3
2
1
12
11

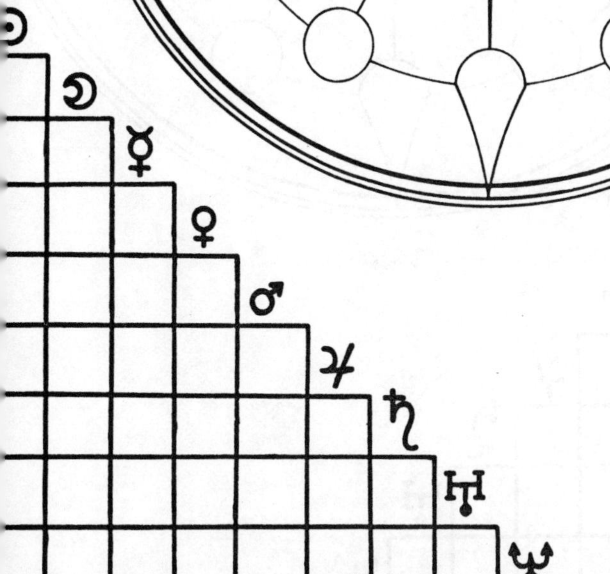
☉
☽
☿
♀
♂
♃
♄
♅
♆
♇

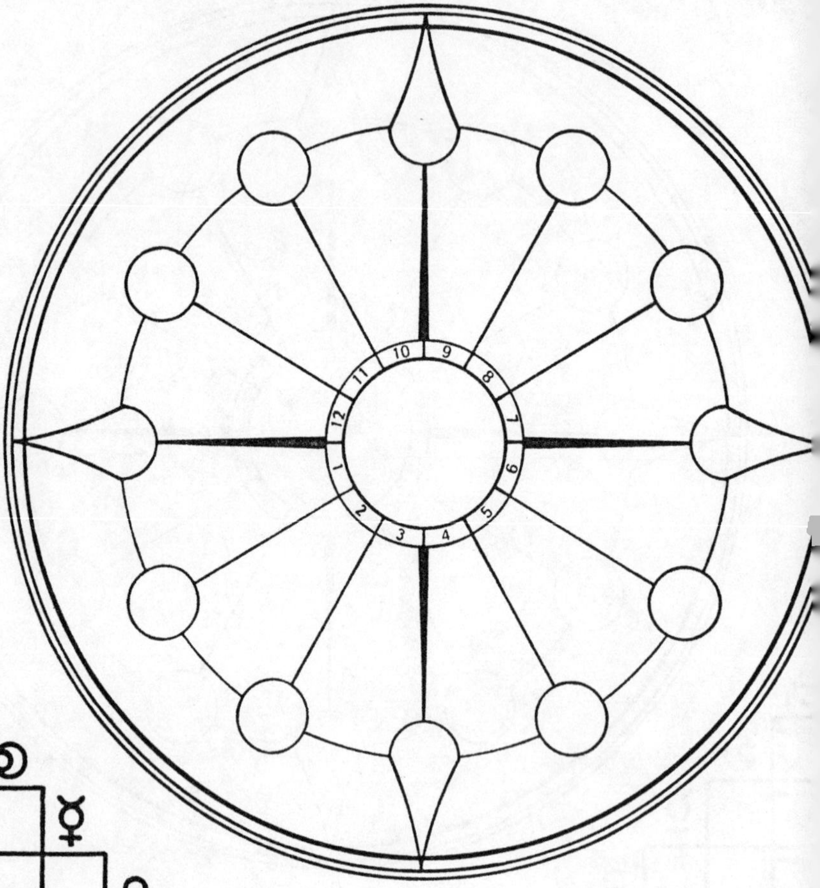

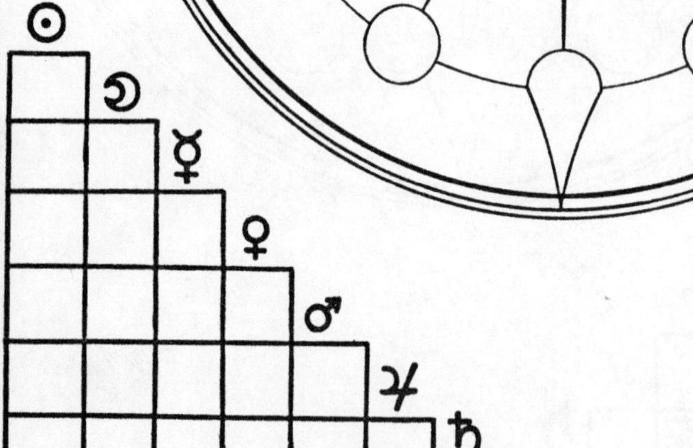

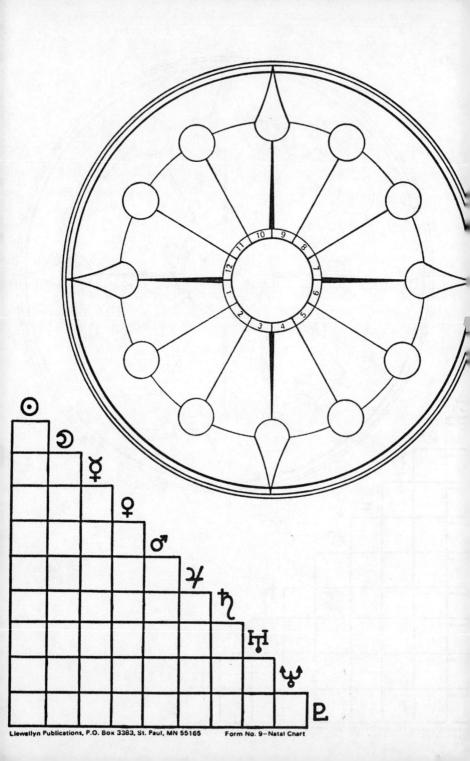

Llewellyn Publications, P.O. Box 3383, St. Paul, MN 55165 Form No. 9—Natal Cnart

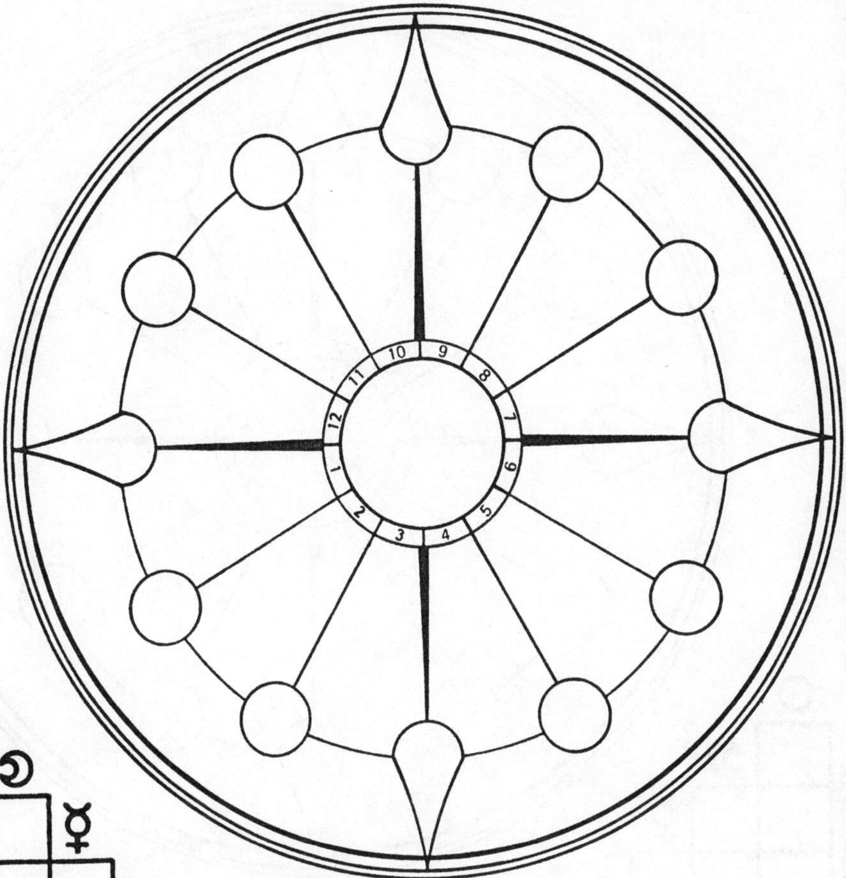
10
9
8
7
6
5
4
3
2
1
12
11

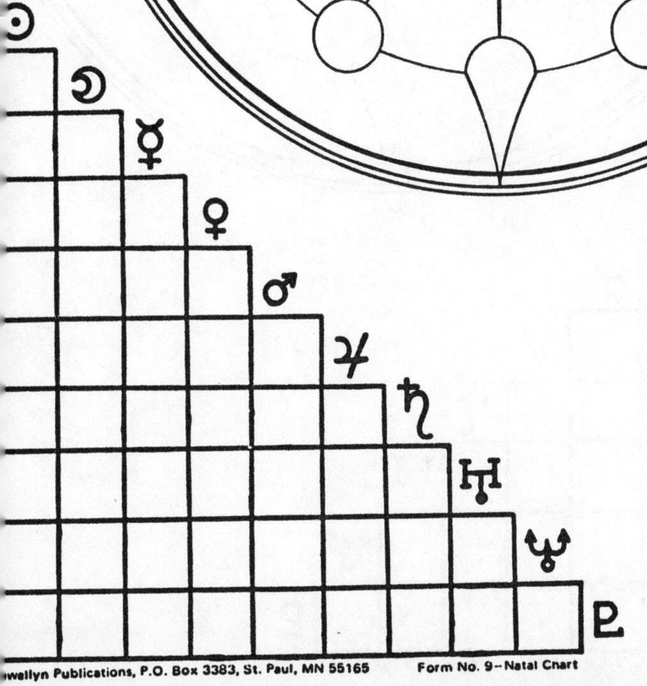
☉
☽
☿
♀
♂
♃
♄
♅
♆
♇

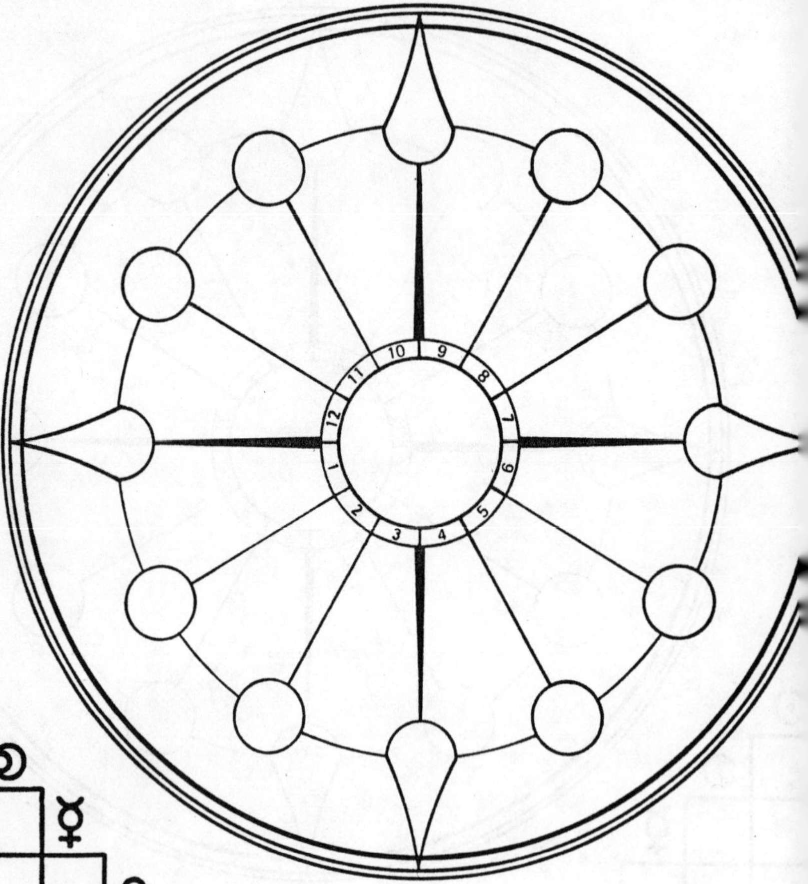
10
9
8
7
6
5
4
3
2
1
12
11

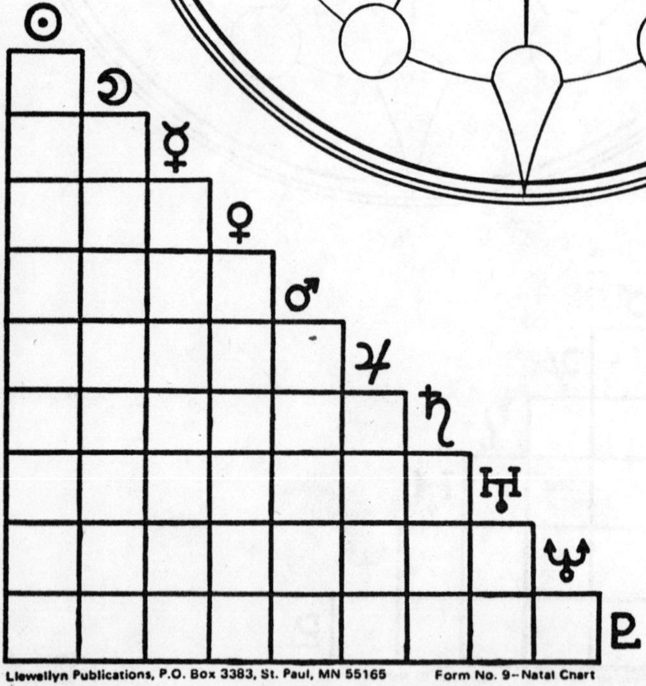
☉
☽
☿
♀
♂
♃
♄
♅
♆
♇